# Alabama Listening
# in the Cold War Era

# Alabama Listening

*in the*
*Cold War Era*

*a memoir by*

## Susan Shehane

Coosa River Books • Deatsville, Alabama

Published by
COOSA RIVER BOOKS
368 Sugar Loaf Hill Road
Deatsville, Alabama 36022
www.coosariverbooks.com

ISBN: 0-9785401-0-7

Library of Congress Control Number 2005908434

Cover Photo © 2006 by Brian Gates
Design by Foster Dickson
Copy editor: Laura G. Harris


Printed in the United States

# Acknowledgements

When I first began writing the book that follows, I had no idea how many persons would become involved.

Without the Sun Belt Writing Project at Auburn University, there simply would not have been a book. I'm grateful to all my colleagues, especially Alyson Whyte, Cathy Buckhalt, John Pennisi, Kim Jones, and Jordan M. Barkley, who is now Assistant Professor of Secondary Education at Jacksonville State University.

I'm equally grateful to Alan Gribben, head of English and Philosophy at Auburn University Montgomery; writers Linda and Earl Fisher of Prattville, Alabama; the Autauga/Elmore County Writers Group, Bob Lee; Libby Bruce, Carole Borowski, and Karen Powell, friends and colleagues in the Autauga County, Alabama, school system. Without the support of all, this book would not have survived.

The love, support, prayers, and friendship of Pastor Henry Lewis Smith have sustained me for many years, and without Henry, I could not have made the journey that became the book.

Dan Waterman at the University of Alabama Press guided me through numerous revisions of *Alabama Listening* (originally called *Alabama Cold War*) and seemed to understand it more than I did. Moreover, I owe a measure of gratitude to the anonymous peer reviewers with the University of Alabama Press whose suggestions and professional criticism helped me bring the book through its eighth, ninth, and final revisions. I sincerely regret that the University of Alabama could not publish *Alabama Listening* in its present form.

I'm equally grateful to Sandy Huss, who teaches creative writing at the University, and who chose the central story of the book to win the Alabama School of Fine Arts' 2001 Teacher's Award for Creative Nonfiction

Susan Shehane

I am especially grateful to Foster Dickson, a colleague who teaches at Booker T. Washington Magnet High School in Montgomery. Foster's professionalism, encouragement, editorial expertise, and experience made the final stages of publication possible. Foster also did the layout, cover, and design.

Most of all I am grateful to all of my family, especially my husband Dwan and daughters Stephanie and Allison. Stephanie and Allison spent many hours editing, discussing, and analyzing raw manuscripts, while Dwan and my whole family were forever my captive audience, sometimes involuntarily. The time we spent sharing the stories orally – indeed remembering them – is a legacy in itself, one I hope we'll treasure for life and share with our grandchildren.

With love, Susan

# Contents

Alabama Listening
in the Cold War Era

## Philippians 1

I thank my God upon every remembrance of you,
Always in every prayer of mine for you all making request with joy,
For your fellowship in the gospel from the first day until now,
Being confident of this very thing, that he which hath begun a good
work in you will perform it until the day of Jesus Christ . . .
And this I pray, that your love may abound . . .
unto the glory and praise of God . . .

According to my earnest expectation and my hope,
that in nothing shall I be ashamed,
 but with all boldness, as always,
 so now also Christ shall be magnified,
whether it be by life, or by death.

# Preface

A group of teachers, along with students studying to become teachers, sat at the table of the Sun Belt Invitational Writing Institute in the summer of 2001 at Auburn University. At the front were Cathy Buckhalt, Alyson Whyte, Art Belliveau, and John Pennisi, all organizers of the annual writing project funded in part by the National Writing Project.

"Institute is a misnomer," I told my husband Dwan after the first few days. "It feels more like group therapy – and I'm surrounded by grown people who've brought Teddy bears, their favorite tea cups, and photographs of their dogs and grandmothers." Dwan and I laughed together.

Grown people, Teddy bears, tea cups. The ambience took me back to the 1970's.

Cathy modeled what she tried to create for her own middle-school students in Opelika: a comfortable, accepting environment in which students could be inspired and feel safe enough to write freely. And so, as she had for over twenty years, Cathy opened the annual writing institute for teachers in the same manner as she had begun the school year for her students, with warmth and acceptance. By the second day of the institute, the adults, who were to be students themselves for six weeks, warmed to Cathy's invitation. Many brought hand-painted memorabilia; some, quilts that belonged to a grandparent; and others, pictures. Many items were a focal point for the teacher-student writers who wrote for an hour each morning as soft music played in the background.

I felt like an uptight outsider. Though I had indeed been touched by Cathy's invitation, by the many tea cups, pictures, Teddy bears, even jewelry, I resisted the invitation. Nevertheless, I secretly responded and held something very dear to me in my purse. I just couldn't let anyone see it – it didn't seem to fit the mold of what I saw before me. My item of comfort and inspiration others would find morbid.

Not until the second week did I bring out my "comfort" item – a small metal box containing the last items my father carried on this earth: his wallet, his L&N pins, his driver's license, and several other items. My mother had secured them in a familiar cigar box in his room five years before when Daddy had been placed in a nursing home. Now, for the first time, I opened the door to Daddy's room, a few months after his death, and I knew that there was much to be learned and shared.

Finally, I mustered the courage to share my morbid little box.

And so it was at the Sun Belt Writing Institute that my colleagues, particularly John and Cathy, gave me the permission to open the box, to unlock doors, to examine the joys and the pain and face the truth that lay hidden behind my father's life, and my own. That was the birthplace of this book, a book I discovered I had really been writing all my life. Pieces of letters, journal entries, childhood diaries, fifteen-year-old essays – all found their way into the book. Other truths I discovered painfully did not appear in print, but I faced them anyway. And in so many ways, this process has been the most difficult undertaking in my life.

For some, this book may be especially painful as we recall growing up in the 1960's in Alabama, when racial tensions reached a peak. However, I think it's important for everyone to acknowledge the era, the difficulties we faced as the South resisted the Civil Rights Movement. I want to apologize in advance to Edgewood Academy, which has grown into a well-recognized private school in which academics are stressed and students experience success in a variety of ways. This is nearly forty years later. We would be remiss, however, if we failed to recognize that many private schools in the South were created to avoid desegregation. For further reading, I would recommend Harvey H. Jackson's *Inside Alabama, A Personal History of My State* (University of Alabama

Press, 2004). Mine is not a political book, but a reader wanting to gain a better perspective of the history of the era and of Alabama in general should certainly read Jackson's book. I would also recommend reading Stephan Lesher's *George Wallace: The American Populist* (Addison-Wesley, 1994).

*Alabama Listening* is a narrative memoir, not necessarily historical. Instead, it imbeds a sort of social history of growing up Southern in the inside, and like memory, it isn't chronological. It is rather like the meandering red dirt roads in Alabama, the clay roads that sometimes lead to the highway, to the river, or back in circles. But like the red clay roads of Alabama, indeed of life, there's usually something to be observed and treasured along the way. Sometimes the journey itself is more rewarding than the destination. Hopefully, you'll find something that encourages you to reflect upon your own life and the impact of those around you. So much can be gained by listening, often just to our own hearts.

When we recently finished the last details of building our house on Lake Jordan beside the Coosa River, one lady helping her husband lay sod made a profound observation. "You had to be lost when you found this place," she stated.

"That's it exactly," I thought. For quite some time, my own children had drawn their parallels. "Daddy's building a house; Mama's building a book," my oldest daughter Stephanie commented. And just as my husband and younger daughter Allison were indeed lost when they found this hidden paradise on the Coosa River, so too was I when I began the journey into writing the book that nearly finished me. It was a five-year trek.

The journey was worthwhile. I am a stronger, more thankful person for all of it, as I hope you will be after you've read *Alabama Listening*. May God bless the joy you find in the journey and give you strength to face what you must see. May you find the courage to discover your own story, the one that invites you to become a part of the legacy that's already yours.

# Prologue
## All that Remains

I have finally faced the closed door of the back room. The scent of cedar, cigar, musty newspaper, and Old Spice lingers. You are all that is missing. I see shoes meticulously paired on a vintage metal rack, the maple bed (a wedding gift), khaki pants to wear tomorrow, bed slippers by the night table for early awakening, and the last pair of shoes with no strings, easing the task of putting them on.

On the bed in a box are the only things left: a Velcro wallet in which you kept your last gold crown filling; a driver's license expiring in 1998; a card showing your lifetime membership to the United Transportation Union, member since 1941; a lifetime Amtrak pass; your first jobs, preserved in antiquity – a 1929 work card on which are typed the words "Clewiston, Florida, United States Sugar Corporation." Elsewhere in the box: a record of Civilian Conservation Corps service in 1933; a post card listing dates of annual Alabama gospel singings; a newspaper picture of a derailed train, a wreck you survived. I am reminded of our ties to the railroad, fabled tales of your adventures, the eight-mile bridge near Mobile, and weeklong trips to Flomaton during potato season.

In the folds of your wallet, a dime.

Glancing up, I shift my focus to the open closet. Brown Crickateer suits, painstakingly chosen from the Montgomery Hub, conspicuously are missing. Mama gave them away when we knew you weren't coming home. She realized that this time the stay, though temporal, was permanent. I am moved to touch the clothes that remain, two cotton, plaid shirts, worn to a thin from methodical care at the nursing home. They were gifts, and they remain. Above, Mama's red hat boxes from the 1940's and 1950's. These I do not touch. Not yet.

But this I can handle. Surely I must do the part of the dutiful daughter, the one who faces even death with resolve, quiet assuredness, and above all, practicality. My ascribed role: When no one else can, whether by default or instinct, I am here again.

How did the youngest of your four children become the parent in the family? Was it gradual, or did it happen on December 7 a decade ago: an explosive day now etched permanently in memory. Pearl Harbor Day. How fitting that your emergency heart surgery would happen on that date. How predictable that Mama would have her own crisis of the heart. The two of you would recover in separate hospital rooms, unaware of the location of the other.

It happened that day. Trembling, visibly fearful in a way I'd never known, you reached out to me as you were wheeled away. And I was alone. I held your hands, comforting you as parent to child.

"You're going to be okay, Daddy," I remember repeating as I wondered where the devil Mama was. Later, I learned that she had collapsed in the parking lot. She too had her drama. But at that desperate moment, you did not ask. You trusted me.

Yes, it was that day.

"Susie, I'll give you a dime to clean up the kitchen for your poor little mother. Your sister won't do it for a dime," you used to say. The competition began.

I was the little one. I always wanted a dime.

My sister and brothers laughed and prodded me along.

"I bet she won't mop for a dime!" snickered Michael with a wink.

"Oh, yes I will! I'll mop for a dime!" This was serious business for me. I liked dimes. More importantly, I liked being Daddy's girl, the one he could count on. It was never about the dime. It was a silent agreement I thought no one else understood.

"Help yo' little Mama out," Daddy said, often referring to Gail and me as the yearlings.

I mopped to help my li'l Mama out, and I helped Daddy, too, accompanying him to the garden as he picked butterbeans. Too afraid of rattlesnakes to lean down and reach into the thick undergrowth, instead I ran to the red-clay road to pick dusty blackberries in late summer. Or I climbed the towering hickory by the side porch to reach the wild scuppernongs. My brothers nailed steps all the way up the tree for me.

I practiced the piano on the bet that I would get better'n Mama.

Wherever you went, I wanted to go, 'coon hunting on a cool night near bedtime. I carried the lantern and you, the gun that was never fired. I shook the water oak or blackjack as the hound dogs bayed at raccoons. Or I called and called when the dogs went off on their own hunt. I prayed that Ready would give up chasing beavers through the swamp. He always came back near dead if he didn't come on back soon, and one ear might be clean near bit off, else he had the snake bite; mocassin or ground rattler.

Wherever you went, I wanted to go, turning pages for Mama while she played piano at shaped-note gospel singings as you tapped out the correct tempo for her to follow. She never did, of course. When you led the whole convention, how proud I was. That's my daddy. And when I played the piano, you were equally proud.

"That's my baby playin'," you announced with a grin. The whole congregation clapped and carried on. It was much, much later that I grew to be embarrassed, but looking back I can understand a parent's groundswell of almost unspeakable joy. Such are the moments parents relish.

Wherever you went, I wanted to be because the feeling was so unmistakably mutual.

We sat by night or day on the front porch swing. You knew the words of the whippoorwill. Mocking birds answered your call.

16

I never tired of the tales, yarns about childhood pranks like stealing watermelons with Horace Jones. I never tired of being the yearling, of Brer Rabbit, or learning to watch the moon to know when to fish or plant. I never wearied of hearing how you made $8 one winter by sending raccoon pelts off to St. Louis. And there were stories – of logging, the Depression, war rations, and waiting months afterward for a refrigerator or automobile. Tales of family victory and defeat – how cigarettes killed Uncle Hub at eighty years old, you laughed, and moonshine cost your daddy his family, the farm, his life.

Life was a narrative waiting to be shared. Like Tom Sawyer, Daddy would have enjoyed his own funeral. At the wake, the family waited in small clusters laden with tears and overpowering, cold, cold floral wreaths. I did my part, greeting visitors, consoling family, introducing friends, being the strong one, agreeing that Daddy looked natural.

"He dont look natural – he's dead," I could almost hear Daddy say. He always found humor, even at funerals. My sister, Gail, late again – just where was she on a night like this? And then the part that would have sent Tom and Huck over the rails of the church balcony: Gail was late because of the final detail. She had searched all over town for Prince Edward cigars. And she found them. And she placed two in Daddy's shirt pocket.

"He always had two when he was going to a singing," she said. Thirty years after he finally quit smoking, Daddy would have a cigar waiting in heaven. Gail and Daddy had made that pact, at least.

You would have enjoyed the family gossip at the funeral. Your sisters whispered they couldn't believe your li'l daughters would do something so tacky. They bet Gail did it.

"All right, Li'l Chaps," I could hear you chuckle. "What're my li'l girls up to now?"

After the first stroke, we learned to walk again. And there were other ways I helped, we all had to help, ways we had to forget. It humbled us. Gail reminded me that the Lord stripped Job of everything except his dependence upon Him, but I chose to remember how you laughed when you told about reading Pooh stories to your granddaughter, my daughter, how she couldn't bear to see Owl's house blown away, and made sure you skipped that page. Later, the two of you took communion, and you said she'd always remember, but I remembered thinking even then – no, Pop, it's you who will remember more. And later, when dementia won, you refused communion, though the pastor faithfully offered it each month.

There are good memories, and mixed, and some I prefer to repress, like the day I broke the trust, your first night in the nursing home. You thought you were visiting another hospital, and when you said you were ready to leave, we couldn't.

"What do you mean I caint go home?" you persisted. "You aint gone put me out in some nursing home to die. You let me die in a nursing home, and I'll hont you. I'll hont ever' damn one of you."

The memory became a dream, a memory I had responsibly forgotten until it was safe. In a cold sweat I sat straight up in bed, threw up my hands, and conceded, "You win, Daddy. You win."

Thankfully, you forgot. We both forgot. We grew content, finding relief in the meekest measures.

Some days I'd arrive at four just to be the one to bring his afternoon coffee. Other patients lined the walls in plastic recliners and spoke without looking up, but Daddy's greeting was one of uninhibited delight, of homecoming and pride.

"This is my li'l daughter," he always told patients and aides and preachers alike, as though for the first time. And when my own children came, Daddy sometimes announced their arrival the same way. Embarrassed, they thought he was confused.

I understand now.

I remember your first Christmas at the nursing home. As we gathered around the piano to sing, you remembered all the words to "O Holy Night" and savored the chocolate and punch and attention, while your granddaughters cried self-consciously, knowing something about their lives had changed forever.

Santa delivered soaps and candy to patients. He posed for a picture there with you as you sat in your wheelchair, held steadfast to your punch, and smiled too gleefully. The picture stayed on the nursing-home bulletin board for several years.

Each Sunday afternoon I spent with you, even in the end when your words grew few and the recognition waned. Some days, you wouldn't talk because you didn't want to wake Lois from her nap. There was comfort in the delusion that your wife would never leave you alone.

"Come back when you can," you said each time, as though to any caller on a Sunday. By then, you couldn't remember how I took you for rides each Sunday, took you home, in fact, for at least the day. On the back porch, I read a story you liked, a Mary Wilkins Freeman tale about two old ladies, one blind, one lame, and their escape from the retirement home. Before you fell asleep sitting up, you chuckled and repeated, "I do declare."

You couldn't remember that I took you to see new toll bridges on the Alabama River. And it was always hard to tell whether you liked the cola Icees or excursions better.

"Now, this is sho-nuff some good stuff," you exclaimed. "Boy, hi-dee. Now this is what gets me away from those four walls. You are a lifesaver, Li'l Chap," you said. "If I couldn't get out one day a week, I'd lose my mind."

There came the day when you could no longer leave the nursing home for rides, when even the promise of an Icee drew little response. "Maybe tomorrow," you said.

When you no longer enjoyed company, Mama faithfully visited every day, and I each Sunday. Others found facing the loss of the man they once knew just too painful. Somehow, I knew that you would know I was there, that you trusted me to always be there.

And now, not every Sunday, I visit the place of your final resting, alone again. Not much has changed.

I face the room now, the bedroom you wanted to go home to but never did. Snapshots, fragments of thoughts, incomplete memories, your voice, all come back to me. For the first time, I have opened the door, because someone had to. It is okay now. The door no longer intimidates me.

As I leave, I know the reward is always there to be reaped again, for what I find is more than remains. I will never be afraid.

I took the dime.

# I

## He humbles those who dwell on high.

### — Isaiah 26:5

Daddy waged a private version of Civil and Cold wars throughout the 1960's and 1970's. We lived in the heart of Dixie in Millbrook, just north of the Alabama River near Montgomery.

When *All in the Family* first appeared as a television comedy, the family sat transfixed as laughter riveted from the oak-cabinet box, our first color television set. But nothing about *All in the Family* seemed funny to my sister Gail and me. We didn't laugh at all. Daddy didn't either. In fact, he refused to watch the show after the first episode. Only my mother saw the irony, the truth. I guess it took an adult to appreciate the revelation: Daddy was the Southern version of Archie Bunker, racism incarnate.

As for Gail and me, we were still too much kids, confused, divided, caught in the heat of the Bible Belt and Daddy's strong political opinions, like Archie Bunker's, usually voiced over a fork at the dinner table. His racist views usually went unopposed, even unnoticed, until I realized not everyone shared them. He was dogged in his hatred of blacks, a hatred my mother thankfully did not share.

She never saw herself as racist at all. She was raised in Georgiana, the same kind of Southern town that grew throughout the country in the late nineteenth and early twentieth centuries because of the railroads. I can still remember my father jealously recalling my mother's relative life of privilege – how in the 1920's her family had electricity and running water when, just ten miles away in the crossroads of Avant, folks still depended upon kerosene lamps. My mother thought her background distinguished her above my father. She was the daughter of a preacher who read, and maybe even wrote, books, and her own grandfather had founded churches in the pioneer era of Alabama. She instructed her children never to use the "n" word and to understand that our father was a bitter man. "Don't listen to everything you hear," she told us. Her teenaged sons by then would not listen, but she told her daughters to say "colored" or "nigra." I don't remember saying anything. But I was always listening to both sides and thought maybe Mama was right all along about a lot of things. She understood oppression.

My mother waited on my father as though she were his slave. No wonder she was more sympathetic than Daddy. She understood prejudice and injustice from the inside out. And in so many ways, I felt even as a child that I needed to free her.

Evocable memories of my silent childhood daunt even the present. They begin with nonverbal fear and end with gnawing questions because I knew so little. In the era of the early 1960's I was just six years old when my brothers Wayne and Michael were teenagers. A child's interpretation of a teen's life centers around memories of her parents' "private" discussions, the brothers' late-night or early-morning arrivals, the ominous clicks of the black telephone receiver, the inevitable silence then wails of a mother who had been betrayed. Such are my recollections. Something always triggered the crisis: a brother had been in a fight. Now one of them, or his friends was in the hospital, or in jail.

Mama and Wayne later would talk about the night Daddy refused to get Wayne out of jail. Mama left alone.

Daddy said Civil Rights would start another Civil War, and Mama and Gail and I were afraid, but Gail and I didn't ask too many questions. Very early in life, we learned the code.

We didn't know much, Gail and I, but we were always listening and thought maybe one day we'd understand.

# II

## The Green House

In the shadows of my sister Gail's memory is the fog of the Green House in Millbrook where our lives began, took form.

The place where we spent our early years was a small green house with asbestos siding, so we simply called it the Green House, but the memories are all black and white.

When I look back, I can remember being as young as three, or even younger. Maybe I heard my father tell the story so many times that I adopted his narratives as my own memory. On the porch is the two-year-old Daddy so often talked about, the two-year-old who was content to carry a large toad through the house to the back porch.

"What you got, Susie?" my father asked me.

"Sam," I said, and continued my mission. Daddy always chuckled each time he told the story.

"All right, Li'l Chap," he said.

In the back room of the foggy Green House was the big piano, larger than the room itself, at least in my memory. I would crawl up on the bench and beat the keys, making repetitive sounds that sounded like music to me. No one would stop me. I would pretend to play the piano like my mama and sing for a long time, until it was time for Mama's nap.

Memory is a cloud of impressions, pealed by phrases and fears. The front bedroom of the five-room Green House was a stark room of black and white, my brothers' bedroom, where the bed was never made. On the walls were no pictures, just gun racks and my brothers' twenty-two rifles. They hunted squirrel. The only memory I have of the room is the time I followed Daddy there, holding onto his leg as I pleaded with him not to whip Wayne, a rebellious teenager. Wayne cried as I begged Daddy, "Don't whip Wayne, Daddy." But Daddy shooed me out of the room and whipped Wayne with a belt. For many people, this was just the way things were done then in the 1950's. Daddy never whipped his girls, never laid a hand on us – his own words. It would be years before I even considered the apparent injustice.

Just eighteen months separated Michael and Wayne in age. Gail was my senior by twenty-two months. As a young child, my impressions of my brothers' troubles likely were exaggerated by the differences in our ages. They were ten- and twelve-years older than Gail and me. Despite some burdensome memories, the early years were pleasant. I was happy even though Gail didn't seem to be. Later I would understand that much of her discontent resulted from her poor health, but at the time, I simply didn't understand. She didn't either.

I remember once as we came home from church, Mama snapped our picture in the driveway. As she said, "Smile!" I smiled, but Gail frowned and whined, "Don't take my picture." I told Gail to smile because when she frowned, she looked like Aunt Mae. We still have the picture and the encapsulated mood of the decade, Gail frowning like Aunt Mae. Sometimes Gail points to that picture as proof: parity was lacking very early in our lives. I use it to point out that sibling rivalry never dies, not even in midlife.

In the picture, I smiled, holding the Bible I couldn't read, along with my purse which still held the dime Daddy had given me for Sunday school. I didn't give it in church because if I had, I wouldn't have had the dime Daddy gave me.

How often I have looked at that picture and wished Gail had been smiling, but I can't change that. I have to look hard to find Mother in those early pictures. She never sat down long enough to have a picture made, or she was busy out back washing clothes in the wringer washer. I would follow her to hang out the clothes.

No one had dryers back then. And it would be years before color television or air-conditioning.

My sister's sad face wasn't the only dominant memory from the Green House. When you're the youngest, of course everyone knows more than you. Especially your older sister, so I listened to everything Gail said, particularly to her warnings of imminent danger. She said that at night there were bears and Indians outside so I pleaded with her. "Let me go to sleep first. You watch for bears, Gail."

When Mama heard this, she laughed and said, "The bears aren't outside! They're inside!"

Of course, we didn't know what she meant.

On the back porch of the Green House was my brother Michael's ham radio, a big black box; its life-size antenna, wired from the screen window, topped the house. I often wondered what the antenna looked like from the air. Out back was Daddy's garden where I followed him to pick peas.

How often I have looked back to the very early years of the Green House, trying to remember. Somehow I thought I owed it to Gail to find the same unhappy childhood she remembered. But looking back I saw only black and white in the Green House, and occasional views of the yard. In the fog of the Green House and my sister's memory I saw green, green water and white geese.

The two geese, Miss Pretty Pretty and Mr. Pretty Boy, had claimed our plastic swimming pool as their home. Now, algae covered the bottom and the top layer held a pungent mixture of pine straw and droppings. We didn't keep the geese or the swimming pool very long. After the geese chased us around the yard and attacked our legs and arms, Daddy said they had to go. That was a sad day.

But I looked to the happier times, like when I followed Daddy everywhere. I wanted to be Daddy's girl. I went everywhere with my Daddy, even to the barber shop and Shortie Gross's store in the heart of Millbrook. There I got cheese curls for a nickel. At the barber shop, Mr. Kanpp, the barber, gave me bubble gum. Daddy would lift me up to sit in the big barber chair, where I would swirl around and around until Mr. Knapp had finished Daddy's haircut and shave. Behind the barber shop was a small trailer for Fat Man Eddie. Daddy wouldn't let me go out back. I stayed inside the barber shop where there were regular men, not big fat men like Fat Man Eddie. One day we heard Fat Man Eddie had a heart attack. Took six men to lift him, Daddy said, and the stretcher wasn't big enough.

In Mr. Knapp's barber shop Daddy would tell stories, railroad yarns, Mama called them. And I listened, noting the time between pauses and laughs, a kind of musical rhythm in the way Daddy's voice went up and down and waited just at the right time. Then I watched the big-stripe candy-cane outside go 'round and 'round, and I looked for the end. When we got ready to go, the men would tell Daddy to take his shadow. They said, "You can't dee-nie her."

When Daddy was at work, I followed our Boxer named Topper, or he followed me. Sometimes he would chase the trash truck and the black men were afraid to come in the yard. Daddy said the only buggerman was a "nigger," but Mama said not to repeat him. I was listening, though, and in the earliest recollections I see now the confusion that began too soon in life. I didn't know whom to trust or follow, so mostly I followed Topper.

When Gail's allergies were bad, Topper sat beside her, loyally whimpering, then licking her leg to keep her from scratching. She scratched anyway and the skin was white and peeling. The scars from her allergies are the signs of childhood and those early years when neither Topper nor I could do anything to help her, though we both tried. We just wanted her to play. Early in life,

I developed that keen longing to want to make things right for others in my family.

Each Christmas Mama brought out the Christmas tree candle that had crowned Gail's first birthday cake. Bringing out the tree candle was as much a tradition as Christmas itself – Gail had been born Christmas of 1953. But as much as birthdays and Christmas were traditions, Gail's illness in our early life left its sad, permanent scar, for Gail often had pneumonia and spent many childhood birthdays in the hospital.

When I made my Christmas wishes to Santa Claus and Jesus, I asked them to bring me boots, a baby doll, and Gail home for Christmas. I played nurse with my baby doll, gave him shots just like Gail got, and consoled him, "There, there, now Jimmy. Don't cry. This won't hurt a bit." He still cried and his rubbery body bore the scars of many shots.

I wanted to fix Gail, to make her well. And so I watched and waited and prayed for Santa Claus and Jesus to make things better. Jesus told me I could help Gail if I watched her, so Topper and I watched her. I told Mama what Jesus said, and she told me to keep listening to Jesus.

When Gail ate all the orange aspirin, I told on her. Daddy said I saved her, but I didn't feel so heroic because then Gail had to go to the hospital, and I knew I had done something else to hurt her. I just wanted her to be home so she could lick the spoon when Mama made her vanilla icing. Gail couldn't have chocolate – because she was a lergic and if she didn't get to come home, Mama said Santa would come to the hospital.

On another Christmas, at a Christmas party for Sunday school, Gail ate a Brazil nut, so she had to go to the hospital again. She was is in a see-through tent at the hospital. That time the asthma kept her in the hospital so long that I got to stay with Hazel.

I always liked staying with Hazel, Hazel Liveoak, Mama's best friend who had a son my age. Larry and I would play trucks – he had a service station and a truck ramp too. And Hazel said she had been keeping me since I was a three-week-old baby and Mama nearly bled to death. That time it was Mama who was in the hospital, not Gail, Hazel told me. I didn't know who kept Gail then.

In the mist of my early memories I can still hear Hazel's laugh. I liked her house where there was lots of laughter and Larry and I could play. There were two girls, older than Larry and me, but I didn't play with them – only Larry. We played in the dirt, but not in the street. Hazel said my mama was the sweetest person she knew. Then she'd say, "Poor Li'l Lois. She's got that bad heart, you know." I didn't know. Not then. But Hazel told me not to worry because she had a hole in her heart and could still laugh.

Sometimes as they sat talking in the narrow kitchen, their voices blended. Hazel made Mama laugh – she was the only one who could. One time Hazel had heard something before Mama, during one of those times when she kept me and Larry, and when Mama came to pick me up, I heard Hazel say, "Lois, will you listen ta'this? Can you believe it?" She laughed and clapped. Mama did too, then covered her mouth.

I had found a song and with one finger I played the piano and sang, "Winston tastes bad like the one I just had. No filter, no taste, just a thirty-cent waste."

After that I always played for Hazel and sang little songs I had heard or made up. So often, at least in memory, I was there without Mama. Larry and I just played. Gail had already started school. Hazel said I could go to school in two years, but Larry and I said we wanted to go today.

When we were at church, Gail and I got to sit with Hazel because Mama and Daddy were leading the singing as Mama played the piano. Someone had built a model church that stayed on a table in the back. Hazel said that church was going to be the new Mill-brook Baptist Church, and I told her I wanted to go inside. She just laughed. I touched the steeple. She said if I wanted to go in the church I'd have to put in my dime. There was a slit in the green roof. But I told her Daddy gave me that dime and I was going to keep it.

I would follow the sound of Daddy's voice as he led the sing-ing. As I crawled around the sanctuary, no one stopped me. Daddy stood up on his toes to direct, so I looked up as I crawled and crawled under feet, following the sound because I could not see, following the sound of Daddy's and Mama's voices. I would find them. And when I got to the front, Daddy reached down to pick me up, because I was Daddy's girl. He put me on the bench beside Mama, but I didn't stay there.

Mama said that in the spring when Gail got better we would get on the train and go to Garland to see Granny. We liked the train station, Gail and I. And we liked to go to Granny's. Union Sta-tion in downtown Montgomery was the same place where we had waited for our geese to come in by freight. We didn't have to get tickets because Daddy was a railroader and we had our L&N passes. At Union Station Gail and I stepped over the cracks in the black-and-white-diamond tile. Gail said, "Step on a crack – break your mama's back," but I stepped on them anyway because I was too small and couldn't take big steps. At the train station I wanted to see Daddy's train, but Mama said he wasn't on the Humming-bird. He was on a freight. Still I looked. Gail and I wanted to ride Daddy's train, but Mama said we couldn't ride freights, even though I'd heard the story of how Michael and Wayne played hoboes and got all the way to Pintlala when they were just eight and nine years old.

We watched the tracks, waiting for our train. The sound of the click-click-clicking as it slowed down meant the Hummingbird was nearly there and the closer it got, the more excited Gail and I were, because that meant we were on our way to Garland.

In Garland I could sit on the front porch as Granny rocked and told stories under the chinaberry tree. She said she was quarter Creek Indian and her grandmother was a squaw. She had seven brothers. She called herself a little Indian boy because she had no sisters to play with. She said that when she was a little Indian boy, she had one doll, a China doll that she wasn't allowed to even hold. The doll stayed on the mantel beside the clock. One day, she crawled up on a chair and got that doll off the mantel. Then she threw it across the room and it broke into a thousand little pieces. She never explained why she broke the doll, but that was the way Granny told stories. They were riddles you were supposed to figure out. I told Granny I was going to tell stories like her, but she said I'd have to do a lot of listening first.

Granny had a picture of Jesus kneeling at a door. It was a picture painted on a rough piece of firewood. And there were words I couldn't read yet, but I still wanted to know.

"What's it say, Granny?" I asked.

"Knock and the door will open for you," she said. "Seek and you will find." I thought that was just some more of Granny's Indian sayings – I didn't know yet that it was from the Bible. I told her we played hide-and-seek after church on Sunday nights when everyone was still talking. And that I looked, but I didn't find Jesus behind a door.

Granny laughed at me. So I told her some more. I told her about the toad behind our front-porch door at the Green House. And she laughed again. Gail didn't like that story.

"His name is Sam," I told Granny. "I told you I can tell stories."

I told Granny how I found the songs on the piano and how I sang "Oh, how I love Jesus, oh how I love Jesus." I showed her the song on the white keys and I played it over and over.

"And you know what my daddy said when I played that, Granny?"

Granny just rocked. "He said, 'Will you look at that Lois? I do declare.'" When he said 'do declare' like that, I knew he was really proud, and so I kept playing. Granny just rocked and told me to make sure I learned how to play the black notes too.

Gail couldn't play the piano like I did, but she could really draw. She drew big, big praying hands, and she drew Topper, and Daddy was so proud that he said to send a picture to Granny, but Mama put the pictures on the refrigerator. They stayed there so long their edges curled, because back then Mama fried everything. Even squirrel my brothers had killed.

When I tried to draw hands, I couldn't – I couldn't even stay in the lines. I thought maybe it was because I didn't go to school yet. But I could play and sing, and that was something Gail couldn't do, even if she did go to school and take piano. I told Gail that she just made the notes sound too hard, and I tried to show her, but she wouldn't listen and she got mad. She said she was never taking piano again, and I told her, fine, I would, but Mama said I couldn't yet because I couldn't read.

In the summertime we went to Foley with Daddy while the railroaders hauled potatoes. It was tater season in South Alabama, and in the fog of my early memories I remember the sandy beach road where Mama said I got lost. But I wasn't lost. I was looking for someone to play with – because Gail couldn't play that day. She was a lergic. So I found Mexican children by the water and I played with them. That was the last place anyone saw me, but I didn't know they were looking. I fell asleep and everyone thought I had drowned. Mama tried to ask the Mexican children where

I was, and later she was amazed that we played together when we couldn't speak the same language. But the Mexicans couldn't understand her, nor could she understand them when they just pointed. They pointed up the road, so Mama thought maybe I hadn't drowned. She found me asleep under the bed back at the cabin.

Those are some of my early memories, the fear of having everyone chastise me – and how I thought they were mad that I lost my flip-flop. In tater season, I loved to go barefoot on the hot sand and feel it squish between my toes. That's where I lost my flip-flop. Mama told me not to play with the Mexicans anymore, so I didn't. She said Topper had to stay with me, too.

Back at the Green House, Mama and Daddy fenced the yard so that Topper and I couldn't go off too much, but I would climb the fence, pretending I could fly like Peter Pan. I remember flying over the house and looking down or going up to the clouds to look for Gail and to see what she was doing in school. Daddy said I couldn't fly, that it was my magination.

Beyond our house, beyond our street, just beyond a dark, sheltered forest of pines were the "quarters" – forbidden territory. When Gail was feeling okay, sometimes she would go with me down the path we had worn through the woods. We wanted to see Sandtown, to spy on the blacks, who seemed so far away. They were just a street over, but you couldn't get there from where we lived, not unless you followed the path through the woods. So we sneaked down that path. We just wanted to see the children we couldn't play with. I knew Miss Alice lived somewhere in Sandtown, and I wanted to go, but Daddy said we couldn't. I knew where Miss Alice lived, though. She came to the house many days, and had for many, many years, to iron for Mama and to rock Gail and me. When she was finished helping Mama, we took her home. She sat in the back seat with me while Mama's little Chihuahua,

Chee Chee Pooh, sat up front with Topper. Topper slobbered out the window and barked all the way through Sandtown.

And those were my earliest memories of the black-and-white years in the Green House, where our lives took form. Later, I might see the irony that the house had no flowers blooming or plants growing, that even the yard itself had no greenery, just mounds of pine straw and sand. But not yet. Still, it was there in the Green House that the seeds of our future were collectively planted.

# III
## Cuban Missile Crisis

I was in the first grade, in Miss Mary Cobb's class at Robinson Springs School in Millbrook, when I first heard about the Cuban Missile Crisis. My oldest brother, Michael, was nineteen and in the Navy. He was on a ship, and in the scary hours of the night, I heard my parents talk, and did not understand. I did not know what nuclear missiles were. I did not know where Cuba was, but I was really sad. Daddy said Michael was back in the bay of pigs.

I could only imagine what that was like, because I dropped my flip-flop in a pig pen one time and the pig ate it. My pink flip-flop. I only had one left, and Mama would be upset.

At Robinson Springs we practiced getting out of our desks and covering our heads. We liked to play duck-and-cover. But when we ducked for cover, the girls especially had to be careful so our panties didn't show. Most always we wore dresses.

We had big crayon boxes that had our names printed in big letters. My mother checked me out of school early.

There are always days like that, days you remember just where you were, what you were doing, even what you were wearing. Like the day President Kennedy was shot. I was in Miss Josie Faulk's second-grade class. It was Picture Day, unusually cool, so I had not worn a dress. Instead, I wore a plain, white cotton sweatshirt and black stretch pants that had foot straps. We were practicing making new words from a list of letters when the door opened without a knock.

It was the other second-grade teacher, Miss Ruby, from next door. She said the president had been shot, and Miss Josie cried, which frightened all of us. Then Miss Ruby told all of us not to worry, that we would be safe. Until then we had not been afraid.

So then we got scared and I remember how a classmate, Mary Jo, cried. Miss Ruby and Miss Josie showed us where Dallas, Texas, was on the map of the United States. It didn't seem far away at all. Then Miss Josie pointed out the U.S.S.R. and it seemed a long way from home, so we took the teacher's word for it. We would be okay.

I looked out the window and noticed how the leaves on the oak tree had fallen. Whenever I'm afraid, I look at the trees and think about climbing the limbs and then I'm not afraid anymore because I fell out last summer and it didn't hurt. Even the stitches didn't hurt. Only the shots stung a little bit.

Then I looked at the reading book on my desk. And then it came to me.

"I know, I know!" I raised my hand and blurted out. I guess Miss Josie thought I knew something about the U.S.S.R.

Miss Josie and Miss Ruby looked confused. "What, Susie? What do you know?" asked Miss Josie.

"Around. The word. The new word. I spelled around. A-R-O-U-N-D. Like our reading book. See? *Around Green Hills.*"

Daddy had his own opinion about who had killed the president. I remember the black and white television coverage, how we were watching Lee Harvey Oswalt as police escorted him in the Dallas police station. I remember Daddy said he must have been a Soviet spy. That was when that Ruby man shot him, and I thought it was so strange that he had a girl's name like the second grade teacher Miss Ruby.

Mama said we were watching history, but we were watching television and we were glad – we had no school the day that we got to watch the president's funeral.

Still, it was a sad day. It took a long time for the horses to carry the president's body down the street, the black and white street.

And everybody was black and white. Jackie Kennedy wore a black dress and little hat and a black veil, and little John John had on black trousers. Caroline was my age. I thought about that. Mama and Gail and I cried when John John saluted the horse carrying the president's body. A flag draped the casket.

Daddy said the "niggers and the communists" were going to take over the entire country, and I did not understand. Mama said not to say the "n" word like Daddy. For so many years I tried to understand what the Cold War really was. Because Daddy said that the Cuban Missile Crisis made the Cold War real. He said the communists had nuclear weapons, but they had other weapons too – like Civil Rights. He said the Civil Rights Movement was a communist plot and there was proof in the 1960's – because the FBI had Martin Luther King under investigation at the time he was assassinated. That's what Daddy said. I didn't know what to think about communists or anything. But I always listened to Daddy. I heard everything he said. When you're little like that, everything Daddy says sounds true, because Daddy said it. Mama's words were different but sounded true, too. She sang a song about little ears.

Mama said the cold war started in your heart, in that place in your heart where you didn't trust nobody no more, when you saw everybody as the enemy and couldn't find anything good to say. She would even sing "Ac-cen-tu-ate the Positive," an old song from the 1940's. She said that when you looked for evil, why, then, you'd find it. Just like my daddy, Joe Lee.

We didn't look for evil because we were Girl Scouts. We had something in our pocket that belonged across our face, so the song went. The great big Brownie smile. Mama was the cookie chairman and leader. When we went to Brownie meetings, I noticed the yellow triangle by the door leading down to the basement at the Girl Scout hut. It was the fallout shelter. There were yellow triangles all over downtown Montgomery too, and when we went to get our car tag in Wetumpka, I saw the sign on the Elmore County Court House. I guess people everywhere were ready for a fallout.

I asked Mama when we were going to a fall out and she told all the Brownies not to worry. We would never fall out because we had our great big Brownie smile. On Brownie day we wore our Brownie uniforms to school and whoever had the bucket brought refreshments.

Wayne graduated the year President Kennedy was shot. Daddy said he didn't know how the generation was going to change the world if they didn't give a flip about their education, and Wayne nearly didn't graduate. He got kicked out for throwing firecrackers into the bathroom and for skipping school. One time Wayne got arrested. I didn't know why. All I knew was that Daddy wouldn't get him out of jail, but when Wayne got kicked out of school, Daddy went to see the principal and got Wayne back in school. I guess that was easier than going to the jailhouse.

Wayne's friends had sayings just like Brownies did, only Mama said we couldn't repeat Wayne's. And she said for him not to say it around the girls.

"We're hell. We're free. We're the class of sixty-three." Daddy said they weren't studying the Cold War and communism or Civil Rights or anything but having a good time. I didn't know it then, and guess they didn't either, but some would go to war and die in Vietnam a few years later. Before the war they tested their freedom, racing motorcycles down Highway 143, the road that followed the river to Montgomery. The riverbank was steep. Daddy said the boys ought to know when to turn back home and to stay out of trouble, because they had their little mama mighty worried. He said that highway ran both ways and they ought to follow the river back home. He said to stay on the dry side, Elmore County, where no beer could be sold. Once you passed the Alabama River, Montgomery County was wet.

And while the rest of the world focused on achieving President Kennedy's dream of putting men on the moon, while the 1960s ushered in the Vietnam War, which would make all of us really wonder what Communism really was, while the world nearly ended when I was just learning to read – Daddy grumbled.

He grumbled about working long hours in bad weather, about Lois spending too much money, about the house being messy, about dinner not being ready or cooked to suit him, about the boys getting into mischief, about "niggers taking over everything." And Mama, Mama just sang. I'm glad somebody was singing. Most of all, I'm glad I was too young to really understand the era, but I was listening. So was Gail, even though we kept quiet.

# IV

## Liberator

"To every season, turn, turn, turn," I sang along with Mama and the radio. We were always singing. "If I had a hammer, I'd hammer in the morning." When the 1960's and I were still new, before miniskirts and the Beatles, before the flower child and free love and the loss of innocence, we were all singing along with the Byrds. Before we understood what war protests were, we still knew all the words and sang along. The times "they were a'changing," but we didn't know it yet. Even the first rock-and-roll I remember was harmless. Gail and I played our 45-speed record over and over, even took it to school so that we could hold it and show it off to our friends. Though we couldn't play the Beatles at school, we danced, and sang the chorus, "I Wanna Hold Your Hand," then added the eight bars that stretched our giggles over the far-too-extended syllable.

Music was always there, always helping me chronicle the stages of our lives, the important events of the family and the world that lay beyond it. I think that even as a very small child I recognized the importance of being observant, of recording the details, of noting the changes around me as I tried to figure out my own role in life. And always there was music, a song without words, perhaps, but always a song in the background. It was the voice of my mother, the liberator.

The 1960's brought change elsewhere, but in the heart of the Bible Belt, it would be awhile before we traded our starched cotton for Go-Go boots or miniskirts. In Millbrook girls wore dresses to school and church. At our church, girls were forbidden to wear shorts to Vacation Bible School, the height of summer activities, which began with a parade. We'd line up in cars at the church and caravan through Millbrook singing, "Vacation Bible School is here – tra-la, tra-la, tra-la." Mama sang out the window of the Bel Aire and waved for folks to come along and join.

And join they did. You never knew what might show up at Bible school, some of the ladies said. To the initiated, there was a silent code to be followed, one not every family apparently knew. One day, Hortense Peel, the Bible school director who wore A-line skirts and sat up in church with the green Broadman hymnal supporting the small of her back, frowned and scoffed at two visiting children. She had decided to send home the two "unchurched" girls who were wearing shorts. That was when Mama intervened.

"Now, Hortense, you know there's absolutely nothing wrong with little girls wearing shorts to Bible school," Mama argued. "If you see something sexy about five-year-old girls wearing shorts, then you've got the problem." That was the way she silenced Hortense and brought a measure of freedom to the five-year-olds. After that, we wore shorts to Bible school. Miss Alice ironed them.

And so began the success stories of Mama's battle for the new generation's freedom. She enjoyed telling the story. So did Daddy. "She gets things done," Daddy boasted, but he refused to let her work for pay outside the home. It proved a man couldn't take care of his family, and he didn't want the shame. Besides, little folks needed their mama at home, he'd say. Li'l chilluns who didn't have their mama at home would go to ruin, he said. "Just look at all them criminals, they never had both parents."

Instead of working for pay, Mama energized herself with volunteer projects. She did so for so long, in fact, that she became a Girl Scout district coordinator. She seemed to enjoy visiting homes to determine the fitness of potential scout leaders. Gail and I listened as Mama spent hours on the phone.

"I visited the home yesterday, and you can't imagine the filth. The floors actually stuck to my shoes, and the odor – it would knock you down," said Mama as she put out her cigarette.

In retrospect, Mama was my childhood hero. She was fearless. When the "integration come in," as Daddy called it, Mama urged us to ignore Daddy. Almost in defiance of Daddy, she made a point to include blacks in Girl Scouts. Daddy protested, sometimes vehemently. Whenever that happened Mama tried to create diversions, which she more or less did by singing and trying to ignore Daddy. She had her own code. We learned that code, Gail and I. We learned the silent code and knew that the truth lay somewhere hidden between Mama and Daddy. It would take years to clear our thoughts.

Although she could not stand up to my father, my mother was a person of many strengths, an unusual woman with uncanny habits and skills.

Around the house, for instance, she became the prime electrician and repairman. She would shove Daddy away from any repair project. She learned to repair appliances and had no fear of electricity. "Oh, it's just a 220," she'd say. Wherever Mama had a hand, wires hung perilously from the walls or ceiling. And back in the days when each phone connection in the house meant a separate charge, she wired illegal phones from room to room, even to the outside. I've often wondered what she could have done if she had ever been introduced to a computer.

With everything she did voluntarily to stay busy and feel important, Gail and I observed that she still envied women who were paid for their work They had earned the kind of respect Mama couldn't get at home during the 1960's. Most of all, they had their own money. I remember Mama's sighs – they were the background of a hot day on a sweaty August afternoon in Alabama. After a while, I could mimic Mama's sighs, the way she put out her cigarette, the way she said, "Yes, sir, yes Josephus," to my father. At the time, I didn't really know what I was doing. All I knew was that my comedy routines could make everyone laugh. And that made things better, and I could make Gail roll with teary laughter. The comedy routines were only done in the absence of Daddy, though. Somehow, I knew he wouldn't find any humor in my charade.

When I said, "Mama, you could have a job if you wanted it," she disagreed. She said that she had accepted her lot in life, couldn't do any better, and wanted to take care of her girls. I didn't understand. She would sigh and say something to the effect of how she was a house wipe. She said too much and so little. How little I understood in childhood would one day be too clear, but for the time, I was happy to accept the mother I found courageous and witty. She was a woman of what Gail and I called gut courage.

She didn't even wince when she performed minor surgery on herself. She could remove fishhooks from her own leg (or the preacher's lip). She rarely conceded the need for a doctor, at least not in time. She never made it to the hospital in time. When every few years she might have a gaping wound, she'd show up about three days too late. "You've got about a six-hour window, Mrs. Lee, and you missed it," the doctors would tell her. "Let's just hope that gap will heal up on its own."

It was a line I heard every two or three years. Nothing could surprise me about Mama.

Daddy liked to tell about the time he hooked the preacher in the lip. Mama performed minor surgery on the preacher man, so we called her Doctor Lee. Daddy would chuckle when he told how he'd hooked Brother Strickland like a river catfish, right in the lip. "Biggest catch I ever made, heh," he chuckled.

Although he might not have wanted her to work, although he demanded she wait on him dutifully, my father admired my mother. He was dependent upon her.

My mother was a person who never, ever sat down. In retrospect, I suppose that's why she could boast, as she did, of never weighing more than 126 pounds – even when she was nine months pregnant. She looked like a movie star, like Meryl Streep or Glenn Close. Gail says now we really got shortchanged in the gene pool. I know Gail did, for sure.

Mama's energy was boundless. She took in stray animals and injured birds and nursed them back to health so that they could fly or return to the wild. She was a kind of liberator who could free everyone, everyone except herself, I began to note fairly early in life.

"Yes, sir, Josephus. No, sir, Josephus." She rarely took issue with anything Daddy said, even when he creamed her in front of company. When he came in the door after a week in Mobile, the first words he uttered after, "Mighty tired," were usually along the line of why she didn't have something cooked for him, or why the house wasn't cleaned up, or why hadn't she gotten the little girls to help her out.

He especially took delight in criticizing her cooking. Sometimes she reminded him about cornbread and buttermilk. That was like their shorthand for remembering the poverty of the Depression.

"Mighty right," he would say. Then there would be a long silence.

And when he wasn't looking, I like to think, she may have added a little extra pepper or a dash of sour vinegar to his peas. And she wasn't any too swift about ensuring Chee Chee Pooh made it outside – in time.

I think she took secret delight every time Daddy stepped where he should not have. Daddy said dogs didn't belong in a house, but Mama had her ways with Daddy – and with animals.

Coming home from church prayer meeting late one Wednesday night, Mama noticed something move in the pathway of our car. On the dark country road, the car's headlights gave the only light, and Mama thought she saw eyes reflected in the taillights.

"Slow down, Joe," she said. "Back up. Back up," she insisted as my sister and I sat up from the plastic seat of the Bel Aire.

Protesting, Daddy backed down the hill of the deserted County Road 7, where few cars were met and no cars trailed. Mama's keen eye had not failed her.

"He's alive. He's still alive!" she exclaimed. Fearlessly, she darted to the middle of the dark road to tend to the animal. "It's a dog. He's been hit!"

Gail and I, lacking Mama's courage, sneaked out to witness from a distance the predictable rescue. Daddy continued to issue warnings.

"You better leave 'im alone, Lois. A hurt dog will bite!"

Mama picked up the bleeding animal and instructed my father to open the trunk of the car. Still objecting, Daddy complied. We drove home slowly with the trunk open. Back home, Mama carefully lifted the animal as she told us to get out old army blankets. We did so. We fetched the army blankets, and Mama laid the animal out in the wooden storage shed Daddy had built out back. Too terrified to help, my sister and I watched ten feet away as Mama doctored the animal. It whimpered and bled, but it didn't die or bite.

We were relieved. Dr. Lee's infamous way with the wild was deserved.

Mama fed the dog. She was so very brave. Every day, we watched from the yard. The animal grew stronger. He didn't really look like any dog we'd ever seen, and we had seen quite a few in the country wild, where dogs often traveled in packs. He looked wilder than a caravan dog.

For fourteen days (Daddy counted and continued to caution), the dog stayed in the shed. Each day, Mama doctored him and repeatedly ignored Daddy's advice about the dog with no name. We didn't call it anything.

Thinking back, I should have known it was strange not to name the dog. Anything left at our house over two hours had a name. And all dogs had names. Why, even "Cur" was a familiar moniker.

We didn't say, "Heeeeere, Li'l Cur Dog! Heeere, Boy!" We stayed away.

We didn't call him Cur or Lame Dog or anything. And only Mama went near the animal. She poured the pine oil to him, chopped up aspirin, and mixed it in with table scraps that constituted the nearest thing to dog food we ever fed animals.

And she fed him pure lard, which could cure even snake bite.

Daily, the dog grew stronger. But a strange thing happened. Before long, the animal began to resist Dr. Lee's attempt to administer the pine oil. Pans of food had to be slid toward the animal because he began to hiss.

And growl. And show teeth for what seemed like minutes.

He dared anyone, even Mama, to come near him.

Mama tried to get the dog to leave the shed, but she had no luck. We all called, though we didn't know just what we would do if the varmint responded.

"Lois, you better stay away from that animal. He's wild," Daddy advised. But what was she to do? The time had arrived for the animal to leave. He might not want a home in our back yard, and he was certainly no longer welcomed, but it was time to go.

"Confound the luck," Daddy said, retrieving his twenty-two rifle.

"Oh, Joe!" Mama wailed. "Don't shoot him! Don't shoot!"

Daddy was as brave as Mama had been when she first rescued the animal. He went around the back yard, sneaked behind the cinder-block fence a hundred feet away, aimed his rifle, and studied his target carefully. Suddenly, gunfire echoed as glass shattered. Daddy had knocked out a window.

"Dagnammit it all!" said Daddy.

He fired again. This time, Michael's ham radio splattered as oil cans rolled around.

Mama's warnings about the lawn mower were intercepted by a third shot. This time, Daddy hit the target. The hissing dog fell. Nobody moved, not even the dog. We waited to see if he, undaunted by death before, would defy it once more. And we waited.

About two hours later, Mama finally garnered the courage to face the task which lay before her. Somebody had to retrieve the dead dog.

"Won't you just dig a hole for Mama?" we begged Daddy, who said nothing. We felt Mama had been betrayed. We were innocent bystanders in this ordeal, but someone had to rescue Mama as well as the carcass of the animal she'd hope to set free in a different way.

When Daddy stubbornly refused to do anything else heroic that day, I raced inside, as instructed, to get Mama a Glad trash bag. Trash bags were very new back then, heavy and thick. Then I found the shovel for my mother. Silently, she performed the task, shoveling up the limp dead dog as I tried to hold open the bag. Gail ran off somewhere, and Daddy too had vanished.

We decided, the two of us, that rather than bury the animal in our yard where we would be reminded of its death for a long time, we would take it off somewhere, elsewhere, down someone else's dirt road. That's what we did. It was near sunset when we finally had the dog in the trunk of the car. We drove three miles until we found the perfect kudzu ravine. Working quickly, like common criminals, we raced to get rid of the evidence. Then we sped off in our dusty Bel Aire, leaving a cloud of dirt on the red clay road that soon covered our tracks.

And then a funny thing happened on the way back. Just as we turned onto the pavement of County Road 7, we both spotted him at once.

It was a speckled white puppy with hair as course and cute as a baby goat's. He seemed to be waiting for someone.

"Aawww!" this was Mama again. "Isn't he cute, Susie? Somebody's just put him out." I knew this routine, if not the dog.

Mama's enthusiasm was contagious, though secretly I had the eery suspicion that the wild dog we'd just killed had been reincarnated.

"It's a mutt," Mama said as she examined the puppy's markings. "Mutt!" Petting the puppy seemed to erase the memory of the recent crime.

We kept that dog for many years, we did.

When I think back on the 1960's, I can remember the kind of mother anyone would want to have; an adventurer, an animal lover, a liberator, a person looking for hope in an era which otherwise might have held only the fears of unrest, and in a home which often held subtle discontent. "To every season, turn, turn, turn," Mama sang along with the radio. Thank God somebody was singing.

# V

## Shaped-Note Song

Above the voices of the congregation at Millbrook Baptist Church, I could hear both Mama and Daddy sing. Gail and Wayne were always embarrassed. They said Mama and Daddy were too loud, and Gail might later even joke about what harmony really meant. Michael could and sometimes did sing along, even though he always had better things to do – like take apart radios or television sets. Our back porch hosted an assembly of giant bulbs that Mama had to step over to get to the wringer washer. Michael would tell how anything was made, but Gail and Wayne didn't even pretend to be interested.

Michael could even explain the science behind musical notation, or how the piano hammers' felted strikes against the strings produced sound. Daddy bought a set of Collier's encyclopedias, and Michael read them. He learned algebra by himself and carried along a slide rule. Still, he couldn't play the piano, I thought, not like I could even at an early age. As the youngest in the family, twelve years separating Michael and me, I always felt like my ear for music gave me an advantage in some ways.

I was always listening.

As a child I was far more interested in the sing-along than Michael's long explanations of circuit boards or transistors or how the piano produced contrasting sounds.

When Mama and Daddy sang above the rest, I smiled and walked closer to the sound, to hear my parents' sometimes offbeat melody. I could see Daddy at the front of the church, standing on his tiptoes, his arm extended to sustain the highest notes. He was the song leader. Above the entire congregational singing, whether in church or at a shaped-note convention (the all-day singings my sister despised) rang my mother's and father's voices.

Each wanted to be heard.

As Mama played the piano, I crawled beneath the bench to watch her feet. The right foot controlled the damper. I watched as she pressed it just slightly after the four-beat counts my father waved, up, down, across both ways. One day, I would learn to direct like that, I promised myself.

Daddy preferred the Broadman hymnal to the Baptist, because the former had shaped notes and the latter, round notes. Daddy was a shaped-note singer, something you didn't find too much in town, even a town as small as Millbrook. But my parents came from the very rural south, Butler County, Alabama, where the roots of their pioneer legacy were formed when the state itself was still so very new. In rural churches like Oak Grove at Avant, my granddaddy Countryman had taught shaped-note singing schools. Indeed, Mama's daddy had taught my own father the seven symbols that would give him a voice that allowed a small group to sing four-part harmony without the aid of a piano or expensive formal training.

In the weeklong events known as "singing schools" the men would sit on one side of the church or community center, and the women, facing the men, on the other. Each group learned to sing notes on a scale by recognizing the symbol instead of the note. In fact, the group would sing the symbols before trying to sing a song.

Now and then one can still hear the distinct, unaccompanied "fa-so-la, re-mi-do" tunes wherever Sacred Harp is sung, more or less as a novelty. It is a heritage worth preserving. It recalls a time when, across the rural South, shaped-note schools and singings were social events, especially during the Depression when many had little to sing about. The schools and conventions served a unique purpose in rural communities and crossroads where many didn't have modern plumbing until the 1960's. Voices of the young sang out about promise. Their shaped-note singing was the voice of expectation, their future, and surely everyone needed something to sing about. As the older men and women listened, the songs helped them forget they had no jobs, that food and medicine alike were scarce, that three of their children had died with the croup or dysentery. Shaped notes and singing became the very symbol of hope that a better day was a'comin' in the sweet by and by.

The church, its wooden frame rising taller than the adjacent corn-fields that formed a picturesque border, was the unifying symbol of promise where the young could gather in their Sunday best to eat, flirt, and sing in that way only the young can about the future they knew would be theirs.

The legacy speaks when silently I visit the cemeteries at Union or Oak Grove, or Mount Olive at Owassa where so many infants, children, and young soldiers are buried – Granddaddy Countryman's family among them.

And so I know now why the church held the promise, why the voices needed to be heard. They still do.

I think about the grandfather who died before my birth, how he gave so much hope, how he taught shaped-notes to people like my father, and even Hank Williams; how my own parents had met at Avant, a community so seemingly distant that the train passing through the heart of Georgiana, eight miles away, barely could be heard.

Teenagers giggled as Daddy moved closer to the congregation at Millbrook Baptist Church, his left hand holding the Broadman, his right moving up, down, over, across and back. Sometimes Gail covered her face, embarrassed. But I heard my father's song. I heard the voice of the accompanist, too, and long before I picked up the pen to chronicle our lives, I heard the story.

I listened as my parents sang and played and voiced their shaped-note songs.

Daddy said I had perfect pitch.

Somewhere along the way, I began to understand that what I heard and observed was more than convention gospel music. Somewhere along the way, I knew that there was so much more, and so I grew up listening.

I listened as my parents sang in their often tinted voices that struggled to be heard above the rest. More than just music, more than being a product of the era, I saw that there was a whole picture of which I was only a small part. Silently, I was becoming an instrument. Later I would see that playing the piano for my parents to sing was in itself a metaphor, not that we shared the same music, but that deep within us we were all searching for the words, wanting to be heard.

And so I learned to listen to the stories Daddy told, to the silence Mama held in response. I wanted to be their instrument, to become a storyteller like my father, the father I liked best when he was telling stories that made us laugh. He was the father we could love, the one we wanted to hear. I vowed to play my parents' songs, their stories, their often dissonant harmonies.

I held onto each note, word, impression, story. While I looked for the words, the story was already forming. Later, Mama and Daddy would make sure I had the formal music training they never had, but though I would reach a new world of Chopin, I would remember the shaped-note song of my parents and grandparents, stories and songs that so very much shaped all of us who grew up listening in Alabama.

# VI

## Joe Lee Tells the Story of Granny's Picnic

The voice of my father spinning tales became a song in itself. Often, my mother would storm off to the kitchen when the rhythm became apparent: Daddy was going to tell another, and this one, Mama might not like. Story time usually came on the porch after supper. It was a ritual that gained strength, through the years, and even my children became familiar with Pop's yarns. One of our favorites, told only a few times when Mother wasn't listening, was the story of Granny's picnic.

"Now, your Granny Countryman," Daddy would begin . . .

"Granny got her that 1957 Chevrolet, got her driver's license, now, didn't learn how to drive till she was durned near sixty. But she'd get in that car and drive all the way from Garland to Millbrook down Highway 31, no more'n forty miles an hour the whole way, 'bout seventy-five miles. On a two-lane road, now. She was a road hazard, I tell you. It'd take 'er all day to drive from Garland to Millbrook.

"She was a sight. Now Lois, she don't like for me to tell nothing on her mama, but I'll tell you  little something. She was active in the Temperance Movement, Granny was, and never would drink a drop, so she claimed. And married to a preacher man down there in Butler County, taught shaped-note singin' schools all over the place. People come from miles around to go to one of Brother Countryman's schools, they did. Granny, a preacher-man's wife, I tell you. And him, ol' Brother Countryman, a Baptist preacher and a Revenue Officer during Prohibition.

"She was gettin' on up there. Now this was many a year after Brother Countryman passed on, a'course. Well, she had to come on up here so's Lois could straighten her out. Now you tell me who had the problem. She didn't drink a drop a'liquor, but she had that old Serutan, I think they called it, that old brown liquid in a quart size bottle, and she drunk about half a pint a day – for her heart, now mind you. Yeah, ol' Granny gone drink that Serutan for her bad heart when there weren't nothing wrong with her 'cept she dipped snuff and smoked s'long she couldn't breathe. And she'd fuss about my cigars, she would. I told her to go on out to the porch if she didn't like the smell.

"Lois took that Serutan way from her, and when she did, why ole Granny, she had reglar fits. She did. That ol' stuff, it weren't nothing more than 80 proof alcohol. Temperance Movement. Heh.

"Why, I 'member a time I caught her standing up in a chair, climbin' up in the cab'nets. And I says, 'Granny, you wont me to look for what you need? What you lookin' for?' An' she told me she was lookin' for her medicine. Bad heart, heh. So I told'r Lois throwed that mess out and offered her some of my Old Hick'ry. She durned near spit on me an' I laughed.

"She was a sight. Bad heart. Heh.

"Lois don't like me telling this. I'll tell you anyways. After Granny got that '57, why one Sunday afternoon, her and Ben, Lois's younger brother, y'know, decided they'd take'm a little ride an' go on a picnic. They took Tippie. That was Granny's li'l dog – she went everywhere with that dog, even the doctor's office and the grocery store – and off they went to a picnic somewheres down there on the outskirts of Garland or Georgiana, maybe on off the other side of Pigeon Creek for all I know. And they took 'em a bottle of whiskey, Ben did, anyhow, and I don't know if maybe Granny'd fried'm up some chicken or not, but off they went with that little dog on a picnic. Just the two of them, heh, heh, and that durned dog Tippie. Lois don't like me telling'bout this, I know.

"They was going to have a picnic. And so they did.

"And they picnicked and they picnicked s' more and I guess they must've got pretty near plastered 'cause 'round 'bout dark time they headed on back to Garland. But they forgot one thing. They left the dog Tippie. Didn't even miss'm till the next morning, and law, did Granny cry. Ben did too. They took that '57 and tried to find the place where they'd done the picnicking and they wasn't none too sure, but I guess they finally fount it. An' so they looked. An' they called. An poor ol' Granny, she cried and Ben cried too, and they spent durned near another afternoon looking for Granny's li'l dog, but they never could find'm. So 'round 'bout dark they give up an' come on home a'cryin'.

"Picnic. Temperance Movement. Heh. I got a kick out of that, but Lois, she don't like me telling none on Granny, the preacher's wife, you know. But by then Brother Countryman'd passed on, you know. Poor ol' Granny. Heh. Family secrets. Tonic. Heart medicine. Nerve medicine.

"Granny and Ben had picnicked s'much they forgot the little dog. Never did find'm. Reckon that's why Lois bought Granny that nasty ol' inside dog, Peanut. Chihuahua. Good fer nothing. Caint house train'm a'tall."

# VII

## Glory-Bound, but Car-Sick

While the world around us changed in the 1960's, Mama and Daddy sang. After all, it had gotten them through the Great Depression, something we heard about so much that we began to feel guilty about having plenty of food. Gail used to joke about Joe and Lois Time, which somehow fell years behind. Daylight Savings Time.

Growing up in Alabama we felt stuck in a time warp with my parents and their singing buddies, as we called them.

After all, no one we knew spent Fridays, Saturdays, and Sundays singing "convention" music or traveling to the most remote country churches down two-lane, winding, hilly, untraveled roads. In normal homes, in my estimation, parents didn't sing shaped notes or wait for new Stamps Baxter songbooks to be printed twice a year. Their homes didn't literally rock from the gospel beat on Friday nights. In later years, Gail and I would insist on meeting our dates by the mailbox on the dirt road. Or we'd run outside to the porch, hoping our dates would not hear the living room alive with foot stompin' and singing that didn't really sound like anything we thought anyone had ever heard before.

As children, we felt all other children got to experience the first movies on TV – "Friday Night Movie" – in black and white. But not at our house, where singings were a weekly event. My parents had their shaped notes, and their friends who read shaped notes, and carried a list of annual gospel singings. The list would read something like, "October-5th Sunday, Maple Springs." And there were other familiar rural church names, like Antioch, or New Hope, or New Harmony. There was never any "First Church of So and So," because we rarely went to any towns where such formality might be necessary. We went to communities and crossroads.

Directions for finding these remote crossroads weren't necessary because the ritual had been practiced for so many years.

At the gospel singings, all the men were called Brother Jim or Brother Joe or Brother Smith, if they were older.

Gail and I never minded being hauled off to gospel singings because that meant we didn't have to go to preachin' at our home church back in Millbrook. Sometimes we'd even skip Sunday School, and when Mama's friends criticized her for taking her children out of church, she reminded them that we were worshiping. Gail and I did worship. We worshiped Mary Campbell and Coca-Cola. Mary, wife of the quartet's bass singer Ray, was the epitome of elegance. She gave Gail and me sample perfume bottles and embroidered handkerchiefs. She wore store-bought clothes, Act III, from Loveman's in Montgomery, didn't smoke, smelled good– lived in the historic house of Alabama's first governor's brother– had a purple bathroom with dainty little soaps she didn't use– laughed gently at everything that was said, and had souvenirs from nearly every World's Fair.

The Campbells had everything – even color television – long before anyone else. Later we would gather in front of the wall-length console to watch the first moon landing and the Lawrence Welk Show with its colored, fluttering bubbles.

We loved going to the Campbell's. Mary talked about her shopping, her travels, even meeting Miss Tillie for lunch at the Elite. The details bored Mama, but Gail and I loved to hear them. Daddy said Mary's daddy had been the bank president in Opp or Andalusia, and she'd come from a lot of money. She pampered Gail and me with cases of Coke – a staple we were denied at home, by the way – free access to creme-filled chocolate cookies, and other perks, such as the promised stop in Troy for "coffee" en route to Spring Hill. That meant Coke and doughnut to Gail and me.

Spring Hill, somewhere near Troy, I believe, was always a favorite singing. All the way to Troy, Mary would anticipate hearing Miss Dixie play. She'd talk about her so much that it almost seemed like Mama got jealous. I liked hearing the red-headed "Miss Dixie," whose ten fingers covered the entire keyboard when she accompanied the convention singers. And she'd turn sideways and smile when she played. I always wanted to play like that, you know, sing sideways and smile and bounce around all over the keyboard like the fat lady in the Happy Goodman Family singing, "You're invited to the country ju-a-ba-leeeeeeeee."

The ride to Troy wasn't uncomfortable, and the distance was relatively negotiable. What I dreaded were those long trips to North Alabama on winding, two-lane roads. In his 1965 Lincoln (the doors opened backward), Ray would drive 70-miles-an-hour, and we'd swerve and swoop. I could feel the car sickness creep up on me, but I'd try not to say anything because everyone was in such a happy mood. Still, I never wanted to throw up in Mary Campbell's Lincoln, so I'd sit up in the back seat to look where we were going. Having a focal point helped a lot. Eventually, I'd ask to sit up front to avoid being sick; then I'd crawl over the seat. Sometimes we'd have to stop for me to throw up, but never once – you can ask Gail – never once did I throw up in Mary Campbell's Lincoln. I'm sure that was a source of great pride for my parents. It was for me.

To the uninitiated, a country gospel singing might sound like any church service. Before the singing, there were typical prayer requests. Somebody would verbalize the absence of another singer, tell us why, pray for them, and then announce upcoming singings. Each singing had a ringleader – sing chairman or director, I believe the term was. And it was that chairman's job to sort of keep things moving. After announcements and prayers, why, the chairman would have everyone start by singing a familiar hymn, a warm-up of sorts. And he'd call on someone to play. There were always several women, and occasionally a man or two, who could play the piano. And so the director would call out the number and after a rather diminutive start, singers were called on to come up, pick the song they wanted to lead, and choose their piano player. Gradually, everything got a lot louder than before. You could set your watch by the volume. Mama was chosen to play a lot. She enjoyed the attention but would throw up her hands, laugh, sigh, and feign fatigue as though to say, "I guess I'm the only one here who can play the piano."

Now, in a convention singing, one side of the church is reserved for the men, and another for the women. At any good singing, at least a third of each side would be filled with singers. The rest of the church would be filled with spectators, people Daddy said couldn't sing a lick. Mary Campbell was one of those, but she listened attentively and earmarked the pages of her favorite songs. Occasionally, someone from the congregation would call out a request, never by name, but by page number.

And before long, when the singers got warmed up and the piano players had loosened their fingers up a bit, you could feel the beat of the music for miles as people would pat their feet collectively. In a country church built off the ground, the sound of that happy stomping was sometimes overpowering. Gail and I never stayed inside very long. Mostly, we stayed outside, explored graveyards, and drank Coca Cola until we thought we would be sick. Once we saw a snake come out of an abandoned grave site; swore we could see bones through the cracks of the molded cement. Graveyards were a keen host for our imaginations. We'd pause to quietly observe infant graves. There were so many.

At other times we'd have rival wars with other singers' children. We always imagined we could just treat them any way we wanted to because we'd never see them again. We pretended we were civilized "city folk" who had absolutely nothing in common with the rural element of Alabama. We could not imagine why we had been dragged out to the country with our foster parents.

Hiding from the truth was, of course, a mistake. We saw the same children either the following week or year at another singing and had far more in common with them than we ever acknowledged. Still, we refused to talk to them, much less play. We were better than they, we mistakenly thought. Sometimes, I think about all those children I could have known.

Many country churches, especially in rural, remote parts of North Alabama, had no indoor toilets. There were separate outhouses for the women and the men. The lines were long – all the way down the hill to the church – the odor pungent and unforgettable, and the flies oversized, blue-green, shiny, and incessant. Women, many big, big women wearing floral print dresses and no stockings, fanned themselves as they waited in line. They would fan and swat, fan and swat, and the fans they carried sometimes advertised the name of the convention with a two-tone, green-and-brown picture of the church.

One of my favorite singings was held each year at the Chilton County Courthouse in downtown Clanton. It was a big convention, Daddy said, and there was plenty to do – plus there was indoor plumbing. People came from all over. Gail and I didn't stay in the courtroom very long. Instead, we opened doors, peered into jury rooms – why, once, I even examined court records, evidence, and parole information. At age nine!

"Sweet little girls," Mary always commended Mama. "They're just precious, and so well-behaved." Gail and I would simply smile. "Out of sight, out of mind," always seemed to be Mama's philosophy of child management, and we could certainly stay out of sight.

Just to appease Mary and Mama, Gail and I would occasionally go back inside to pretend we were listening, and I'd pick up a song book and actually sing along. Sometimes I played the piano with Mama. She liked that. Together we could make the piano sound like a player piano, but Mama would get faster and faster, and I just couldn't keep up with her. And whenever she finished, she'd always laugh in a sing-song kind of way and exclaim, "Weeeeeeeee," like some kid riding a bike downhill with no hands. The closer to lunch time, the louder the group got, until it just had to break. Lunch meant tables and tables covered with cold pole beans, fried chicken, pecan pies, and mysterious casseroles. Gail wouldn't eat anything. Afternoons featured "quartet music," so that the rest of the singers could just take a little "quiet time" after lunch. That's when the Millbrook Singers would sing, and from time to time, I'd either play along with Mama or play for the quartet myself. When I played by myself, Mama would invariably call out corrections, or Daddy would beat out a different tempo. Most embarrassingly, Ebbie Barrington, the lead singer whom Gail always said looked like a jack-o-lantern, would announce, "And playin' today is Li'l Susie, Lois and Joe's daughter. She's just ten years old."

What I liked about the convention music was that the four parts would answer each other. Sometimes, the bass might have a solo line filled with a fast run of dotted sixteenths – "I'm going to take a train on the glory express," or something. And the altos and sopranos might respond together, "I'm heaven-bound." Then as tenors might respond, Daddy's voice would be louder than anyone's: "Won't you come and join me as we travel on?" And then everybody might sing, "We'll wear a crown."

There was always a train, somewhere to go, and a crown to wear, to be sure. And, of course, there was always someone waitin' on the other side of the pearly gates.

The crowd could only take so much hoopin' and hollerin' and stomping their feet, though, so usually after an especially spirited song, someone would request a slow, 12/8-tempo song, "I'm headed for heaven," or something. In a song like that, part of the melody line was always repeated, "headed for heaven." "Someday I'll see Jesus" ("Yes, I'll see Jesus") and so on. Gail said the songs all sounded alike, but if you listened closely, you could tell the tempo was different, and the mood, too. The slow songs were all about sorrow and grace and having a reunion in the sweet by and by.

Shaped notes – once I tried to teach Daddy to read "real" notes, as I called them. I drew the staff, and I pointed out that all he had to do was to look at the lines and spaces. But he never did. He much preferred looking at the shapes of the notes, and that, I could never get. They all looked alike. Mama could read both shaped notes and round notes, or so she said.

The two of them would argue over a tempo or a note anywhere, as though they were a comedy act on the Ed Sullivan Show.

"Now, ol' Josephus, you know that's a *do*, not a *fa*," Mama would almost sing.

"Fa-so-la, re-mi-do," or something, Daddy would sing. He seemed to understand completely, and he wouldn't bend, at least not in the beginning. Eventually, he would concede Mama was right – she always was – and the whole congregation would laugh or Ebbie would throw in the punch line. Gospel singings, jubilees. Happy, heavenly, glory bound on the railways to heaven. "Turn your radio on," the song went, "and let Jesus come in."

Mama wrote music sometimes for the regularly published songbooks, like Stamps-Baxter. I remember the quartet singing her tunes, tunes like "Get thee behind me, Satan" and "When He calls me, I will answer Him. Listen, yoo-hoo, Jesus is cal-ling you." It was her own answer, I suppose, to the Avon commercial of the times. If you listened closely, you could even hear the doorbell. Gail hated that music and would get as far away as possible so she didn't have to listen. But you couldn't help but hear it.

Happy times, until I turned thirteen and learned what it meant to be embarrassed, and I simply refused to go back. Ebbie seemed to forget that I was no longer ten, and his announcements about my age made me want to hide.

Instead of going to singings, I stayed home – and once, at age thirteen, actually drove my brother's 1966 Chevrolet Malibu all the way to Prattville to visit a friend. Michael had mistakenly taught me to drive at the same time he taught Gail, who was old enough by then to get her permit. I stacked up volumes of Sears and Roebuck catalogs to sit on, and just took off. So many years later, I can still remember the difficulty I encountered keeping the car in the road along the steep McQueen Smith Road. I could imagine being tossed into the kudzu-covered ravine and never found since no one knew where I was. But I went on. My friend told her dad I was much older than she was, but neither of us could have weighed a hundred pounds.

I got back home just in time. The singing was over.

And so for years, I almost never knew there was a Cold War. At least we could pretend, Gail and I.

# VIII
## Threats

I see now that the gospel singings I later refused to attend had served as a cushion in an otherwise frightening era. So many years later, I would look back and long for the innocence of creme-filled cookies, Cokes, cold fried chicken served on long tables behind a country church. There were so many  matters that weren't so frivolous, and to a child growing up in the South in the 1960's, life held a series of surprises from which no one was exempt, not even children, especially Joe Lee's.

As a child growing up in Alabama in the sixties, through Kennedy and George Wallace and Martin Luther King, Jr., I was aware of the political divisions that Daddy said threatened  another Civil War. Vietnam, the Voting Rights Act, Bobby Kennedy, evangelists like Billy James Hargis, communism – all fused in my memory of the sixties, and as a child, I had difficulty distinguishing them.

But they were always there, and Daddy did nothing to shield us from them. We became political parties in our own right, secretly raving for the poll taxes which Daddy said would block "nigger voting" in Alabama.

"You ought not to say that around the girls," Mama always insisted. By that time, Mama had begun to do her own ironing, having lost her veteran domestic help who'd been part of the family for as long as I could remember. Always  round and cheerful and loyal to Gail and me, Alice began to speak up to my father. She quit working for us one day during a  national news broadcast of one of the riots. Later,  I heard Daddy say, "She gone to De'troit." Alice's family did move,  but she herself remained in Sandtown, the black community near the gravel pits in Millbrook, caught between the Civil War and the evolution of Civil Rights in the Deep South. Mama visited her alone. She would tell Gail and me, but not Daddy.

When I think back now to my mother's secret visits, I see a person who had lost a friend she wanted to reclaim. Alice knew my mother's life. She knew what it was like on the inside, in the home of Joe Lee, away from the gospel singings, away from the church crowd gathered after evening service to hear Joe Lee yarns in the parking lot, away from the Girl Scouts. Alice knew my mother not as the Scout organizer, but someone torn secretly while keeping her family together, shielding her daughters and sons from the world that lay beyond, from the Vietnam War that threatened to include Wayne and Michael, from the Civil Rights Movement that threatened to claim all of us as its seeming victims – and most of all, from her children's father, her husband, Joe Lee. Perhaps he was the greatest threat of all. We didn't know at the time. But so many years later, I know that Alice knew. Alice and Mama had something so very much in common: they were victims of the Deep South and men like my father. There really was no escape. I know that now. Perhaps Alice knew so then.

The threats of the sixties became real, real when Alice left, real when we watched the black and white television that in memory seems to chronicle the changes that so shaped our lives. I can still see President Lyndon B. Johnson declaring war on poverty. Daddy would snicker and call him a "nigger lover." But Mama never laughed with him. Instead, she reminded him of the Great Depression.

"Remember what it was like to be hungry, Joe? Remember?"

Daddy never acknowledged the comparisons. Instead, he would talk about how welfare would ruin the country. He said Lyndon B. didn't know beans about "niggers," since he came from Texas.

"And everybody knows they aint no 'niggers' in Texas," he

would say. "And besides, they's so outlantish that they even de-clared theirselves they own country. Did you know that, Lois?"

Mama's silence was the only response. I remember that so well. Although I had not begun to write about my mother or my father, by the mid-sixties, so very early in my life, I'd found the best silent friend anyone could have, a diary. Each day I addressed it fondly, recorded the day's most important events, like Chee Chee Pooh's birthday, or the fact that Gail had had another asthma attack, or when Granny was coming up next. Later, I might think how Granny was another silent friend. She just rocked and listened and occasionally uttered something that I might now see as some sort of inherited Creek Indian wisdom. But not then.

There were other things to observe then. Along with the rest of the world, I watched the 1960's unfold with each day's evening news. Now that I teach middle-school-age children, I wonder about my preoccupation with world events as a child. But at the time I thought everyone was engrossed in news. Every day we counted the "casualties" of the Vietnam War. I didn't understand what was meant by the term "troops," and so I asked Daddy. He called them political fallout and said our boys didn't have no reason to be over there fightin' somebody else's civil war. Since his own sons had reached the draft age, he'd toned down some about communism. He said there were enough wars to fight without goin' afar.

    I still remember sitting down to watch Chet Huntley and David Brinkley – the 1960's and 1970's all one blur of fear and black-and-white photo memories. Each day brought evidence that Daddy was right about all the wars to fight: All around, life was threatened. Another city on fire with riots. Birmingham bombed. Nigras marching from Selma to Montgomery. Daddy told us about the bus boycotts and how the "niggers" had taken over the city pools, so Montgomery closed its pools. And so much more.

I remember Daddy's daily commentaries on a predictable strain of topics – poll taxes, George Wallace's promise from the steps of the University of Alabama, "Segregation today, segregation tomorrow, segregation forever." Everyone had pictures of George Wallace and his wife, Lurleen, who became Alabama's first and only female governor. Then she died. Her children were my age.

To those of us who grew up listening in Alabama, the loss was personal, even for children. Grief permeated the entire state as though our own mother had died. We stayed out of school and watched the black-and-white television coverage of the funeral. I was forever intrigued by Chopin's "Funeral March" as the hearse took Lurleen's body down Dexter Avenue, so I learned to play the piece on the piano, almost as a way to revere and recall the feeling of the great sadness everyone shared. It was like the day Kennedy was buried. Caroline was my age, too. So many children, I thought, with parallel, yet unparallel lives, caught up in the era of the 1960's and in the lives of their parents. Later I would think of the Nixon girls, also so close in age, and wonder how they felt when their father faced the nation and the world to resign as president. But that was a few years away yet.

We were still caught up in the world of the threatened South, certain to face another civil war. My father rallied against the Civil Rights Movement.

That is, until Martin Luther King, Jr., and Attorney General Bobby Kennedy were shot down. The prospect of civil war became too real then, not just a political point Daddy could make as the evening news made the latest threats clear; not just a remark made at a family gathering, or outside the church on a Sunday evening.

Daddy became ominously silent after Dr. King and Bobby Kennedy were killed. I don't know if he had second thoughts about his beliefs, if he was simply worried about the impending civil war, or if he thought the whole matter was a communist threat. Certainly, someone was to blame.

At that point, too, even as an eleven- or-twelve year-old, I began to see the world as a different place than the one my father saw.

And I wondered about the blacks who had lost a leader. I empathized with the Kennedy family and thought of so many children without a father. Perhaps for the first time, I understood Mama's silent war, the war that sided with the oppressed, the war that silently fought for the rights of all people, not only of color. But women like herself.

A new fear arose.

It seemed all great leaders were destined to die, and we were all afraid.

My father silently became a sworn deputy for the Elmore County Sheriff's office so that he could have a permit for his concealed pistol, which he carried on his weeklong trips to Mobile.

Later, he liked to boast about the time he nearly used it. As a drunk swaggered toward him one night by the Princess House Diner along Government Street, Daddy pointed the gun underneath his coat pocket.

"Now that's far enough," he warned. Immediately the drunk sobered, turned around, and walked straight away from Daddy, who always chuckled when he repeated the story.

In later years, we left him alone on my daughter's graduation night in 1996 because he was too embarrassed to use a wheelchair in public. Mama arrived late that night to find him sitting with his pistol pointed and loaded. When I learned of the incident the next day, I took away the gun. Daddy fussed so much that I gave it back, but without the bullets.

"Now you're like Barney Fife," I told him. "You can have your gun, but not your bullet."

"All right, Li'l Chap," Daddy laughed. In those later years, he liked being Barney. A small brown cup that says Pop and contains Daddy's bullets is now an heirloom at my house. Each time someone picks it up, I can tell the story. I have become fond of my role to preserve the stories that shape the pasts and create a link between former and future generations.

When I look at the cup and rattle the bullets, I can remember the fond stories and still know the truth about Daddy's pistol and civil rights.

Daddy? He was "agin' it."

As for me, I learned the balance Mama couldn't fathom. I learned how to love Daddy without hating him. I was Daddy's girl.

# IX

## Hickory Hill

As I had even as a very young child, I looked to the woods for comfort, strength, serenity. Ironically, in the troubled era of the 1960's, my parents moved outside Millbrook to a ten-acre plot that Mama named Hickory Hill. Even in an era that otherwise brought fear, the woods held a secret serenity for all of us, except perhaps Gail, whose allergies kept her from enjoying the outdoors. Where she saw no life at the dead end of a dirt road, I saw adventure, comfort, trees to climb. Tall hickories and mounds of unraked leaves healed the waters of those troubled times.

There are always those points in memories, those symbols of an age.

Like the watch Mama gave me. When I turned twelve, Mama gave me my first real watch, a windup, silver-plated watch that had twenty-one jewels, a symbol, perhaps, of things she thought it was time I was interested in. And she forfeited her sewing room so that I could have a room to myself – even installed a telephone extension in my room – all to encourage me to take up the interests of other preteen girls.

Daddy wouldn't give me a rifle like he had the boys ten years before, but we drove three hours that Saturday, nearly all the way to Lineville, Alabama, to pick out the handsomest black-and-tan hound $75 would buy. My own hunting dog.

It was the highest form of acceptance a father could demonstrate to his youngest daughter, even though I knew the dog – like a good fishing rod – was more for Daddy than me. Yet, I felt I'd earned his respect, and even that of my mother and Gail, whom I hoped would envy the kinship Daddy and I shared for our love of the outdoors, for late-night 'coon hunting in the hills and swamps, areas they wouldn't dare venture on a cold night.

And so it was that fall we began training Rough. At first we would take him out only with one other dog, our Walker hound, Ready, so named for his insatiable appetite. Ready was the best, a good runner – wouldn't go after squirrel or rabbit – and he seemed to take up for the black-and-tan. Whenever Rough would stray for a 'possum, Ready patiently would lead him back to the right scent.

On days Daddy was in Mobile, we fed the dogs and let them run a little. Sometimes we kept them penned, not because they might be killed in the traffic: there was none where we lived, not even a highway. There were only miles of red clay roads with few farms spread in between.

Instead, we kept them from running squirrel and rabbit and going off on snake hunts, though snakebites weren't uncommon. Sometimes when we'd hear a flock of jaybirds and know a snake was nearby, Daddy would let the dogs out just to find it. Not only would they find it; they'd fight until either it was dead or had bitten them. Sometimes even that didn't stop them. We'd feed them pure lard then, if a snake ever got them. All afternoon we'd feed them lard and make them drink water. Next morning, they'd be swollen, but we never lost a dog to snakebite. Sometimes Mama heroically went off on her own with her chihuahuas and hoe to fearlessly hunt down the moccasin and ground rattlers.

That winter Daddy and I spent many nights in the Elmore County hills, in the swamp beyond the spring twenty acres below our house. We'd head out at bedtime, always with a compass, light, and matches. In the woods like that you learned how to fend for yourself, how always to find your way back by marking trees or following the creek. You learned lots of things, how to say what you wanted without speaking at all. You learned how not to fire the gun before the dogs were ready. You learned to follow a bay for miles, and to know when it was time to turn back.

Sometimes we left the dogs fighting beaver in the swamp. They might not run rabbits, but they'd all challenge the beavers. It was always a fierce contest, too, and we knew calling 'em wouldn't work. We just headed home and prayed they'd return more or less in one piece. I remember once when Ready returned all beat up, his ear barely hanging to his head. I was always afraid next time it would be my hound puppy Rough who was still cuddly and cute – like a stuffed toy. Ready was weathered and scarred from years of chasing animals who sometimes bit him.

We didn't do too much shooting. Most times, we would shake the tree, the 'coon would get away, and the chase would begin again. I held the lantern. That was my job. It wasn't so much catching the 'coon as running it that was the adventure, anyhow.

I still have the watch, pictures of the dog, and memories of those late-night hunts. I think of them often as I take the interstate home and pass the Millbrook exit where a sign commemorates Hank Williams. The Lost Highway follows the Alabama River, where the bridge overlooks the distant swamp and moss-laced water oaks.

Mama said when we moved to the country outside Millbrook I could ride my bike for miles, so I did. I went exploring too.

Sometimes I would ride to the highway, nearly a mile along the narrow dirt road where trees hung overhead. There, in the strangely cool spots in the red dirt, I felt the clay between my toes. I tied my shoes on the bike handle and parked my bike like it was a horse. Sometimes Gail and I or the twins up the hill went all the way to that place down County Road 7 where an old tree struck by lightning eons ago had wild pink roses growing all over it. There I could imagine we were De Soto's group first discovering Alabama, and we had found just the right place to settle for the day, a palace of pine straw. Sometimes we would pretend to be Indians. Granny said we were Indian, and I imagined I looked the part with my dark skin and hair, but not as much as Granny with her long hooked nose.

Whenever we went exploring, I didn't wear the watch Mama gave me. Gail said I didn't need to anyway. She said to just watch the sun, that Girl Scouts could always tell time by the sun. That was easy in a life in which the only real boundary we knew was dark.

Sometimes I was very adventurous and went alone. Moss hung from all the trees in the swamp, so I couldn't tell which way was north, but I knew the way back home was south, and I could always find my way. If I followed the water, I could always get back home. And if I listened to the sound of hounds bayin', even across Kenner Hill, I could tell the distance. I knew the dogs would always find their way back home and all I had to do was to follow their sound.. They never got lost. Neither did I.

We would follow the spring around the hill. I loved the smell of the spring water near the bay trees, how the area by the water was so green. Sometimes the dogs and I shared the same spring water. The water was so cold, so absolutely pure and sweet.

The twins up the hill, along with Gail and me, found the Garden of Eden below the far hill just the other side of the swamp. A pure natural pool where the sunlight comes in over the trees and you could actually swim because the water's so deep. No one else knew about our secret paradise. We could always find it again because we bent limbs down along the way, like the good Girl Scouts we were. When we went back, we went northwest of the swamp and across a big field I didn't know was there. Tall, tall Behera grass, so tall it was like hay, and brown from the heat of the summer. I stepped on a black snake and ran home, leaving Gail at the bottom of the field.

As I got off the school bus in the afternoons, I would smell the hickory and think that winter must not be far off.

But Daddy had said Gail and I weren't going to public school next year when I would be in the sixth grade. In fact, he said we might move to Australia to save us from integration and Civil Rights. But he had said that once before, and it was just like the time I got saved at church and told everybody I was going to be a missionary. It didn't happen. I knew we were not moving to Australia as much as I knew I was not going to be a missionary. And If I had to go to the academy, I would. I bet nobody there could play the piano like me. I hoped nobody would remember I was supposed to become a missionary, because I was really going to be a concert pianist. Someday when I played, people would whisper, "That's Joe Lee's daughter."

And I was going to be Miss America too. Gail said, "What makes you think you could be Miss America?" I told her because I was pretty and could play the piano. I was prettier than her and she knew it. Gail told me I was stupid and ugly, that I would never be smart enough to go to college, much less become a concert pianist. But she conceded I could play the piano all the same.

On Hickory Hill I preferred riding my bike to practicing the piano sometimes. Frequently, I rode two miles down the main highway and stopped off on a nearby dirt road, the one that led to Thornfield School. I climbed a hickory tree by the road and studied the old home place that doubled as a small school for Millbrook's elite. From the tree near Thornfield, I could see all the way to Montgomery, past the Tyler Goodwin Bridge. I could see the dome of the state capitol.

I never got too close to the house at Thornfield. I stayed on the dirt road just this side of the hill, and I just stared, because this was the place, the same hill where a writer lived. Her name was Childs. I couldn't figure out why a grown woman was named

Childs. But I had read her book of poems from the library and I wanted to meet her and tell her I was a writer, too, but she'd never believe me. I wanted to tell her, but I was too embarrassed to venture any closer. Besides, I didn't know what I'd say if she asked me what I wrote about or wanted to write about. I was still looking for the words.

She wrote poems about being a ballet dancer, but I didn't know anything about ballet, or dancing. Still, I had written little books in compositions notebooks for best friends, made-up stuff about girls who got to go far away from Millbrook. And so I remained too embarrassed to meet the one person I felt I really wanted to be like, a writer, someone I didn't know at all.

And so, I wrote anonymously to my diary.

*Dear Diary,*

*Gail got baptized in Mr. Sarber's goldfish pond in Elmore. She had on a purple skirt and a white shirt, and when Brother Gordy dunked her, you could see her bra and her whole shirt just glued to her. I'm glad I got baptized before I needed a bra, plus I got baptized at church, not a goldfish pond like Gail.*

*Mr. Sarber built the goldfish pond himself. I guess he could because he owns Sarber Monument and makes grave markers and little benches for people to sit on when they want to be near graves. All the time in the building right next door to where he lives. It sinks down, just like the pond. Must be sad to have to build headstone out of rocks and have to talk to all those people crying all the time. I would not want to have to see sad people every day. And I've never known anyone dead except Uncle Claiborne in the fourth grade. I thought he was going to just sit up — he looked asleep. Wake up, Uncle Claiborne. I just knew he would. And everybody was so sad and crying, only I didn't because I*

74

*knew Uncle Claiborne would wake up and was just asleep.*
*Granny was real sad.*
   *Your friend, Susie*

*Dear Diary,*
   *Sometimes I have the sick headache like Mama, so she*
*shuts the blinds and turns off all the lights. When I try to*
*sleep I just throw up and my head hurts so bad I think I*
*will die. Gail doesn't get the sick headache. But she has al-*
*lergies. She can't even go in the woods with me anymore.*
   *Mama gave Granny a little Chihuahua for her birth-*
*day. Named him Peanut. Daddy cusses the little dogs be-*
*cause they poop on the rug and you can't see it until you've*
*stepped in it.*
   *"Dagnabbit," he says.*
   *Chee Chee Pooh sleeps on Gail's bed. It's good for her al-*
*lergies, Mama said. She said it will cure the asthma once*
*and for all. Daddy said Gail's come out of the kinks since he*
*put in the pool. She aint puny no more, he says. She can hit*
*a home run and she weighs ninety-five pounds. They call her*
*Home Run at school. But she still breaks out and has scars to*
*prove she's scratched all her life.*
   *But I can outrun her, especially on a bike. And she's never*
*ridden all the way to Millbrook like I have. I bet she couldn't*
*find her way back up the hill without me. I'm sure of it.*

And those were the Hickory Hill years, the selective memory Gail
said I developed in order to forget the childhood we really had,
one in which we felt isolated in our rural home, misunderstood by
parents who had no clue how to raise children in the 1960's, different because we attended gospel conventions while others went
to rock concerts.

Looking back, I can see that Gail was right about so many things, how you did pick the memories worth retelling, but I can also see the woods were my shelter even when they made Gail sad. I can see how I preferred my father's funny stories to his tirades about the cost of living, Civil Rights, communism, the Vietnam War, long-haired Hippies, and LSD.

And I can now see how my father's stories shaped my desire to be a writer, and I was listening. We all were.

When I remember the front porch swing of our home at Hickory Hill, I still hear my father the storyteller, the one everyone liked, spinning his yarns.

# X

## Pop's Railroad Yarns

A nd so my father would begin.

"Remember me telling you about Porterfield?

"Well, way back in steam engine days at Pritchard, they was a'goin' down the track 'bout sundown, and they hit a yellow board there at Chapman. That meant the next'un be red, but the engineer, he never did slow down. He just kept a'goin', and he hit the red' un next. Well, he couldn't get stopped, but the old local had stopped, and so they hit the caboose, but before it hit, ole preacher I'm tellin' you 'bout, well, he jumped out the winder.

"Well, now, I went down there to the in-vestigation. Ole Porterfield, he was plastered all over, had two walking sticks, he did, this ole preacher I'm 'tellin' you 'bout. Now the railroad officials, they got him to come up and test-i-fy. They wanted to know how come he had jumped off that train, so he come up and he said, 'Well, I tell you, it was like this – I was of two minds. One of 'em said, "Stay with her, Porterfield." And the other'n said, "Porter, you better jump." And so I jumped.'

"An' he said, 'When I come to, they was a guhl a'standin' there over me, and she says, "Man, is you hurt?"'

"An' Ole Porterfield, he said, 'Guhl, have you got a aspireen?' That's what he actually told in the in-vestigation. That bunch just rolled.

"He was just plastered all over, head to foot. It's a wonder it didn't kill'im. 'Guhl, has you got a aspireen?'

"Ole Porterfield, preacher man, he was. When he first come on the engine with me, diesel engine by then, he told me, 'Mr. Joe, I been a pastor down at Fort Deposit twelve year.'

"An' I told'm, said, 'Porterfield, you must be a pretty good feller if you'n stay in a church twelve years.'

"An' he told me, said, 'Well, I tell you, Mr. Joe. I tell you like it is. I make it my practice – you just don't fool with them women in the church. You know they will talk.'

"Now that's a preacher for you.

"One morning we got ready to leave out of Mobile, and it was a cold rain. Dint matter none. I walked from the front unit all the way back to the back unit. I hunt up my air hose wrench, my hammer and my chisel, and all that 'quipment I'm s'posed to have in case we break down.

"Well, I got back there to that rear unit and I seen there was a big quilt and it was movin'. You couldn't even get in that cab, and I thought for a minute, 'They aint s'posed to be nobody in this darn cab,' and so I punched at the quilt and I said, 'Wake up, henh!' And they was a hollerin and a jumpin'. An' after I poked around a bit I said, 'Y'all caint ride in henh.'

"And two poor-lookin' fellers creeped out from under the quilt and one of 'em said, 'We caint get out of here –  it's a'rainin'.

"Well now, I dint say a word. I just turned around and went back to the head unit and told  ole  J.R. Cranford to tell the engineer 'bout it.

"An' so he picked up his radio and said, 'Send a special agent down here", an' boy he was up there ti'rectly, stopped his car, and went to that rear unit, got 'em, marched 'em right on out and put 'em in his automobile.

"Well, we was stopped at Flomaton at the end of the double track, waitin' on a train, and ole  Cranford was back there lookin' round, says, 'Them two fellers  left a half a'gallon'a wine.' An' ole Cranford come  back up there. I was leanin' back with my eyes shut, like this, you know, and he stuck that wine up to my nose. I jumped up like I was all excited 'bout it, and Cranford, he took it, started to pour it out, when ole Porterfield, he says, 'Wait a minute deh, Mr. Cranford. Don't pour dat wine out,' said, 'I got a friend that likes dat wine.'

"An' so, ole Porterfield, he took that wine with'm.

"There's another thing about that ole preacher. He said he made it a rule long time ago to let his men, when they take up a collection, to always 'start at the back and come to me.'

"He said he was in St. Louis at a big meetin', and they was some kind'a people there, said they had four men taking up collection. Said they was puttin' in some big money. An' he said, 'You know, you know one of them got to the back door and he just kept a'going — y'aint never seen'm no more!'

"Yeah. 'Start from the back and come to me.'

"Now, he had learned to be a preacher man, hadn't he?

"Ole Porterfield, he had a lot of gold in his mouth. Boy, he had all kinda gold. J.R., he was on the engine with me and he got Porter to show'im where his cemetery was. And we was ridin' on down near Greenville, and ole Porter he pointed to a lil'ole place down there off this side of the railroad. He said, 'Dat place right out dere, dat's where I'm gone be buried.'

"And ole J.R., he says, 'Yeah, and when they bury you I'm gone come back and get all that gold out'yer mouth.' We jest kept a'ridin', an' ole Porter, he never said ' nuther word 'bout it. An' he never would show me where he was gone be buried in that cemetery. He thought J.R. meant it. J.R. gone come get that gold.

"You learn a lot about people when you work with'em. I rode the engine with J.R. ten years. And he was worth all kind of money, he was worth a lot of money. He owned over five hundred acres a' land and a ole store. An' all he did was put that money away, boy. He come in one day — now this is a true story — him tellin' me, that's how come I know it — he come in one day an' his wife had drawed all that money out an' put it in 'nuther account in her name. They separated. He said, 'I quit'er.' He finally told'er, 'You'n have that. By, so-and-so, I'll make me some more.' An' they went back together an' he lived with'er until he died. He was the darndest feller y'ever seen in your life. He was so tight with a doller – that's why she drawed it all out. Yeh. 'By God, I'll make me some more.'

"He drove all the way to Montgomery from down at Pine Level for years and dint never have a jack. One mornin' he come in late. He had got about two, three miles down the road and had a flat in his truck. Had to walk all the way back home t'get his car. Come in about twenty minutes late. But he still wouldn't buy a jack.

"You learn a lot about people when you work with'em.

"He had this ole handbag, just everything fallin' out of it. He wouldn't buy a good handbag like I carried. No, he had a paper sack. He shaved with a reglar razor and a shaving brush. I had a nice li'l leather bag I carried all that stuff in, toothbrush, 'letric razor, and everything. An' he had his in an ole paper sack. He carried that ole paper sack everywhere. He come in the hotel an' he laid it up on the counter. Well, Mrs. Stewart, the lady at the Admiral Semmes Hotel for years, she saw that bag – it was dirty too. That ole bag'd been used s'long it was wrinkled and dirty, and Mrs. Stewart throwed it in the trash can. She just thought it was ole rubbish. But ole J.R. , he come back lookin' for his razor ti'rectly, and there it was, Mrs. Stewart done throwed it in the trash can.

"Well, they got it, the paper sack. But she gave'm a big bank bag. You know how these hotels have big bank bags that say Merchant National Bank. He put his razor'n everything in it, and he'd go down Gov'ment Street swingin' that big bank bag. I kept hopin' somebody'd grab that bank bag an' run off with it.

"He was tight, all right.

"You can find out something 'bout people when you work with'em a long time. He was a sight.

"That shore did tickle me when Mrs. Stewart throwed his ole paper sack, razor'n everything, into the trash.

"J.R. died last year. Most pitiful sight y'ever did see, his wife at that funeral, carrying a walker, 'bout ready for the nursing home.

"An' you know, I run into a feller at a funeral the other day that knowed J.R. Knowed him back in Wilcox County. Darned it there warnt a feller there – an' I told'im I put in my lifetime with the railroad, an' he said, 'Well, I reckon you knowed ole J.R.,' and I told'im, 'Well, I reckon I did. Rode the engine with'im ten years.' Said J.R. had two hunnert and fifty acres that joined his in Wilcox County.

"An' he knew all kind'a people from Butler County. Knew all kinda people where we grew up near Georgiana. We used to sing with'em. You get to talkin' – he was kin to one of my best friends, first cousins, I believe. I can get up a talk with anybody, I believe. I can go down there to the mall, you know, get to talking to some feller. First thing you know, he'll tell me where he's from.

"This feller I met up there one day, he was from Wilcox County, an' he was tellin' me what a mess the schools was in down there. He was tellin' me how they got a mess down there. When the integration come in, everybody just turned over the schools, gone off and left'em. Now they got a mess. Blacks – they wanted it whole hog or none. No white people now, not one. All black. Camden, Pineapple. Everywhere down in there the whites done run off an' left the schools – that's the reason they caint get any money. They's a place down there in Wilcox County, or Dallas, called White Hall. They formed'em a little city there during the Civil Rights Movement. They's a hundred something down there – an' boy they have been giving tickets down there on Highway 80 like it's out of sight. Making money. They gone build a mall down there now.

"But they couldn't pay they light bill one month. It was a hunnert and ninety somethin' dollars and they couldn't pay it. What happened, that revenue sharing quit comin' in, and that's what's got'm up agin' it. They don't get that government check now and they couldn't pay the light bill. Ole Governor Hunt, he give'm a hunnert and something thousand dollars to put in city water down there. And they talkin' bout building 'em a mall down there now.

"I think they used that place as some kind of rest stop when King was marching from Selmer to Montgomery. I think that's what started the city off."

Whenever Mama heard Pop's stories, she'd just sigh and complain about "re-runs." But the rest of the family, and later grandchildren, never grew weary of his tales. We yearned for memory of the railroad storyteller. He had seen so much in his lifetime, remembered traveling to school on a horse and buggy. He had witnessed the evolution of the twentieth century as the Model-T gradually replaced the family mule, and sandbed roads turned to asphalt. Like so many who came into their prime at the height of the Great Depression, he had worked in the Civilian Conservation Corps, the "Three C's," part of the Work Progress Administration created by the priestlike President Franklin Roosevelt. And like so many his age, Daddy had enjoyed his part in building state parks, roads, and bridges across Mississippi, Florida, and Alabama.

"Working men built this nation," I can hear him say. Living in tents, camping out in swamplike conditions in the heat of August – "Don't give me none of them 'good ole' days,'" Pop said, chuckling.

Whenever Daddy talked about how men built the country, Mother reminded him that it was Franklin D. Roosevelt who'd been the country's savior, who'd given men work and brought food to hungry families. But Daddy would remember seeing tons of potatoes literally thrown off railroad bins, destroyed to bring up the price of produce. They rarely agreed on anything, even memory, Mama and Daddy.

Later, when they moved to Lake Jordan to retire, my sister made a railroad sign to post on the fence by the entrance to their home The juxtaposed boards read JOE and LOIS. Gail's creation was emblematic of the inside joke kept between secretive sisters. "Wherever they are, there's a crossing," she laughed.

In the distance, I hear trains sound. Their approach to railroad crossings on a two-lane road is always memory, at once a beckoning, dream, vision, lonely recollection of the man I called my father.

"Railroads built this country," I can almost hear him say. He had been there. When he had been hired by the L&N, he must have felt, as he would say, that his train had come in, that he would somehow build a future and be part of it at once. Passenger trains linked small towns, and the railroad could stop at each one, carting not only travelers, but also freight. I also remember when the last Hummingbird passenger train made its final run from Montgomery. We went over to Union Station by the Alabama River, viewed the car's sleek dark green and chrome finish, and marveled at the conductor's trim black uniform and white-trimmed hat. Michael still recalls the Hummingbird train number we caught to travel to Georgiana or Greenville. "Number Six," he says, sounding just like Daddy. And so we watched the Hummingbird make its final run that day. We peered into the dining cars with their starched white linens. Daddy must have known that the day marked the end of an era.

"You take the passenger train out and every li'l town'll dry up," Daddy predicted.

In my dreams I hear the train call and long to hear my father once again tell those railroad tales. Crossing a track, hesitating because of my father's lifelong warnings, I am always taken back and hear that voice, once again, cautioning.

"Now you can't depend on them lights at railroad crossings 'cause the railroad aint reliable no more. Tracks and lights, they're all in shambles. Boy hi-dee, I tell you. More than once I had to pick up a head and arms, not t'gether, mind you, but strewed from one end of the track to nuther. Put 'em in paper sacks like garbage." Daddy would grow silent, shaking his head, as he recalled the most difficult assignment he ever undertook on the railroad.

Michael says that before gates and caution lights, flagmen manned the busiest crossings, twenty-four hours a day.

And so I stop at those crossings now and marvel at the man known as Joe Lee; his preeminence in my life was so clear from an early age when I would follow him around to wait for proverbs or tales to flow through narrative quips. He could sit on the front porch swing, mimic the calls of hoot owls and bobwhites, and have wildlife literally perched on a nearby hickory. We too were called to his tunes, poised on the porch as we awaited his next words.

Mother wasn't so attentive to the front porch stories, however. Instead, she recalled Daddy sitting on a lit cigarette on the swing, the telltale smoke drifting up from the seat of his pants. He could not hide from her the fact that he'd cheated, once again, in his endless endeavor to quit smoking. "That paintin', boy-hi-dee, wear you out ever' time."

In my dreams I am the teacher, overlooking a young girl who says she needs more paper to finish her story. "Just change it," I advise.

She looks up at me, pencil in hand, shaking her head. "But I don't want to." I cannot see her face, but I hear her voice even when I'm awake. I would like to give her more paper, but now I'm awake and can't.

At railway crossings, I wait for the freight trains to pass, marvel at the graffiti, and look for hoboes, but the freight cars are hauntingly empty. On my way to work, a teacher now and always a student, once again I am reminded of Daddy's lessons, how union men in the brotherhood had to strike for regular work hours, health benefits, paid vacation, all the time giving up regular pay to gain improved working conditions. "Weren't none of it free, I tell you," I hear my father say.

And so the railroad crosses my path, as it always has. "Just make sure you stop and look both ways before crossing," I hear my father say. I have heard about the severed heads again. And I wait. I think about writing assignments for my students, how the concrete leads to the abstract, how my father's life was itself a metaphor, and I wonder if I can convey something meaningful to my students. I wonder if they can take something more from what they learn, if only they'll listen.

# June 1967

## Groundbreaking at the Academy

We drove to the clearing by the edge of the woods.
In the heat sweat ran down the back of Daddy's neck,
and my bare legs stuck to the seat of the car.
Daddy chewed his cigar, spat out the window.
Each time he leaned I moved closer to my sister.

The ground was hard by the cornfield, no rain since May.
Pegs were posted like flags, a yellow ribbon tying them.
Daddy said there'd be only four rooms at first.
Might be a year before other folks saw things our way.

Two men in suits stood with shovels.
A young boy carried the state flag as we sang "America."
I thought about sixth grade at the big school,
how I would've played piano for assemblies.

But Daddy says no child'a his can say yessir to no "nigger."
The tall man prayed and blessed the grounds.
We ate cake on a covered table by the cornfield,
gathered sting nettles and bitterweed.

We played exploring in the woods until time to go.
By then tall woods by the field
formed a dark sunset of their own,
near the clearing by the edge of the woods.

# XI

## The Prophesy of Ruination

When the news came in the late 1960's that schools in central Alabama would be racially integrated, both Mama and Daddy were visibly upset, terrified for the safety of their children. Daddy swore, "No childa mine'll ever say yessir to no nigger." His words still haunt me. In my fifth-grade school year at Robinson Springs School, I couldn't find the right words to explain to my friends why I would not be attending public school in the fall. What no one talked about was the fear that the black children must have had, the fear that their physical safety was literally at risk by being among the first to integrate the public schools. They were the true unsung heroes of the day, but my father didn't see it that way at the time. Neither did Mama, who, though she harbored no prejudice, didn't want to involve her children in political affairs.

"Integration will be the ruination of the public schools," Daddy prophesied. He said he wasn't about to let his little daughters be taught by blacks, only he used the "n" word, and he predicted a decline in morals when the blacks and whites mixed together. All Gail and I knew was that we would be taken away from our schools and friends. Forced to attend private schools, we felt as though our world, and in retrospect, childhood, had come to an end.

Groundbreaking ceremony for a new private school, a summer day. Gail and I wore dresses, as was always the custom back then. In the field where the private elementary school was to be built in Elmore, the ground was dark and hard. Daddy said it had been a cornfield. I could not visualize a school in the field. For the first time in my life, a quiet, heavy sadness and anxiety filled me. Gail would have to go to a different school, and we would

87

no longer ride a school bus together, a ritual that symbolized the school experience. I can still remember the smell of the tall bitterweeds on a September morning as we awaited the school bus, taste the dry, red-clay dust that clouded the passage of the few cars on Hickory Road, see the blue sky, the sky that always held promise for me in September.

The promises didn't seem so promising anymore, and for the first time ever, I dreaded the prospect of returning to school. But I didn't say too much. I was learning to survive the cold war.

Gail, who was going into the eighth grade, was really mad and said she was not going to a private school. Daddy said she didn't have a choice. Wayne and Michael were lucky, I thought, because they had already graduated from high school and didn't have Daddy telling them what to do anymore. How I wished that Daddy would just "go with the flow," as Mama always said. But he never could. Besides, I didn't see what the big deal was about integration.

Gail was going to have to go to Williams School in Montgomery, a school she said was for people who couldn't make it in a regular public school. And she didn't want to have anything to do with those people. They were hoods, she said.

It was dark that day we visited Williams School, and I saw what Gail meant. It didn't even look like a school, and many students – who were there even in summer – had bleached hair with dark roots. I agreed with Gail – she didn't belong there. Gail cried, and I cried too, trying to hide my feelings because I knew Mama was sad too.

Looking back, I can appreciate Mama's dilemma – just getting us to school was going to be a challenge. How would she take one child to Elmore and another twenty miles away to Montgomery? Certainly, the way our older brother had gotten to school was out of the question. Michael, who had attended Starkes Military Academy, had actually hitchhiked twelve miles to school each day.

We'd pick him up in the afternoons, sometimes, as I recall. I remember tall magnolias, so tall they reached as high as the second-story porch of the antebellum home-turned-private school. Every afternoon, the young men in their uniforms would end the school day by retiring the flag and saluting. They had a regular drill.

But the few years that had passed since Michael's graduation could have been a lifetime. There was that much difference. Mama said you couldn't turn back the clock.

Integration was going to happen, and there wasn't anything anyone, not even Joe Lee, could do to stop it.

Daddy, and so many like him, fought the ideology. Each day seemed to bring news about court orders. The federal government had become the enemy of the South, but there was hope, Daddy said. The hope was in Gov. George C. Wallace, a former judge from Clio, who vehemently stood up to Judge Frank Johnson. Daddy rallied around Wallace, as did the whole state. But you could not get away from the fear, the fear in the hearts of so many, like my parents – especially Mama. No one wanted to see the innocent become poster symbols for Washington politics. Those words were her banner.

Daddy said the South had always been discriminated against, ordered around like second-class citizens, and he said the Civil Rights Movement was just more Reconstruction. He talked about what he had heard all his life, how after the Civil War, Yankees came down south to give the blacks jobs in government and they didn't have a lick of education, he said. And all of this was nothing more than an economic war, he said, one the South had lost after the Civil War, and people up north were still trying to win. Keeping industry out of the South, even unfair freight charges for Southern runs – all of it showed that the North was still discriminating against the South, Daddy said.

Mama sighed, as was her custom. She said Joe was still fightin' the Civil War and reminded him the South had lost. "There ain't no more cotton to pick" became a familiar phrase.

Daddy said there was going to be another civil war. He talked about Australia again, as he had so many times before – about moving to get away from the Civil Rights Movement.

What would we do if there really was another civil war? I wondered if I could take piano lessons during a war, and would our dogs be okay. And what about Granny? Would the war be like the Cuban Missile Crisis – one where no one got hurt and it was over pretty quickly? A cold war?

"Joe, you ought not to frighten the girls," Mama said. She assured us that no matter what, we would be okay. I believed Mama, more so because it was Mama who was always there, not Daddy. And we were Girls Scouts, always prepared. We were prepared for war, if that was what it took. What I wasn't prepared to do was to leave my school, to leave the comfortable, familiar two-mile trek to the only school I'd ever known.

In the summer, I liked to ride my bike to the school, stop at the Speedee Market for a cold drink – the first canned drinks. Gail and I would ride all over the school, across covered sidewalks, down by the merry-go-round, all across the sandy playground. No one ever stopped us. But it wouldn't be our school anymore. Daddy said we'd hand it over to the blacks.

And all of this because of a few federal judges. This is what life was like in the mind of an eleven-year-old going into the sixth grade at the time.

Private school lasted a year for me, and less than six weeks for Gail who re-enrolled at Stanhope Elmore. There, as elsewhere in public schools, the first year was filled with fear. Parents would hear rumors of planned race riots at school and would keep their children home. There was genuine fear that first year. At some point I liked being at the academy, protected from public school politics.

But I missed my friends back in Millbrook. Each day as Mama carried me to school in the 1960 Chevrolet that symbolized the passage of our lives through various phases, I would look to the left at a hayfield. Beside an abandoned lumber yard, the field was completely clear, with the exception of an oak tree in its center. I studied that oak and decided to silently dedicate it to the friend I missed most from Millbrook, Cindy. From that moment on, I told myself, I would always remember Cindy whenever I passed by that tree, and hopefully she would remember me too. One day I mustered the courage to tell my sixth-grade teacher about the tree, hoping she would ask me about my friend. Instead, she said, "How lovely, Susie, to name a tree after a friend. Are you Indian?"

Confused, embarrassed, I simply said, "No, but my granny is." And that was the end of the tree discussions. Still, I reserved my own moments of silence each day. I didn't tell Mama about my tree. Funny thing was she wrote a song for the new school and we sang it at assemblies. "A Tree Grows in Edgewood," she called it. I don't remember the words, only a few, something about its roots being solid.

But I kept quiet at home and at school. There were greater issues than my own, and though I didn't have the words to comprehend my reticence, something inside told me to be silent. Daddy and Mama were, after all, so impacted by many outside forces. They wanted to protect their children. And there were other concerns, no small part of the era – their sons were in jeopardy of being drafted into the Vietnam War, which Daddy maintained was a civil war the United States had no part in. Wayne joined the National Guard, at that time a way to avoid deployment, and Michael would have willingly gone to war had he been called. My parents had no control over the Vietnam War, but the civil war in Alabama, the new civil war, that was something that still showed the promise of resolve. Daddy was hopeful.

The promise of the future hinged upon George Wallace, the Alabama governor-who-would-be-president. George Wallace had fought Judge Johnson and stood on the steps of the University of Alabama promising "segregation forever." In George Wallace, Southerners could rekindle the states' rights battles that preceded the Civil War a hundred years earlier. Wallace was a powerful man, clever with words, and Daddy quoted him often. For most of my life, Wallace had been the governor of Alabama. And when he decided to run for president, Daddy was so excited – everybody was.

Thus in the early 1970's, victory for the way of life we knew in Alabama seemed imminent as George Wallace gained political momentum. It was not right for little children to be bused for an hour just because a federal judge wanted to integrate all the schools. It wasn't right in Alabama, and it wasn't right anywhere. Busing seemed to be the ticket. All over the country, my father pointed out, people were sitting up to pay attention to the "fightin' little judge" from Clio, Alabama. Finally the nation understood.

Then came that ominous, incipient day in May 1972, the day Wallace was shot as he campaigned in Laurel, Maryland. By then he had a new wife who seemed every bit the First Lady Jacqueline had been, but in more of a country-singer type way. She stood by her man even as he fell, presumably dead, in the parking lot – and wore his blood on her suit all day, just like Jackie Kennedy had. We would see the devastating parking-lot scene repeatedly played on our first color television sets.

The day George Wallace was shot is a day forever etched in the memory of so many Alabamians who were watching and listening, like the day Kennedy was shot. Only Wallace lived. He lived as a broken man, and from that day on, like the day his wife Lurleen died of cancer, a pall fell upon the state. Defeat, again. The centripetal force which had been the very core of the South and my father's beliefs had been severed. Something about our lives changed forever in 1972.

# XII

## Songs Without Words

My father always loved to tell the story of the "miracle." It was the day he believed it had been manifested, though Mama said it began even earlier. At age five, coming home with my family after Sunday morning services at Millbrook Baptist Church, I slid onto the bench of the massive upright piano in our tiny living room. My feet dangling far above the floor, I picked out a few chords on the white keys. Then I began to pick out the tune and chords to "Oh, How I Love Jesus" The family surrounded me as they prompted me, singing along, "Lois, would you come listen to this?" Before long, even Michael and Wayne asked me to play in front of their friends. Wayne joked that soon I'd be playing like Jerry Lee Lewis, and when no one was listening I tried to thumb, "Whole Lotta Shakin' Going On." I never could quite catch the rhythm.

In a few years, when I'd grown tall enough to reach the piano pedals without standing up, I sometimes played the piano for the Millbrook Singers, only to be embarrassed when the lead singer, Ebbie Barrington, announced without shame, "And playin' for us this mornin' is Little Susie, Lois and Joe's little girl. She's just ten years old." My parents laughed and never noticed that each time Ebbie announced my age, I grew more and more withdrawn.

Meanwhile, for several years, I studied rudiments with teachers at the elementary school. In the 1960's, teachers gave private lessons in the dressing rooms of public school auditoriums. Mrs. Hazel Etheridge, my first teacher, a petite lady with tall curls, wore pastel colored shoes. She brought finger-nail clippers to school and made me play John Thompson's *Teaching Little Fingers to Play* until I grew weary. The music I studied was not the music I wanted to play. But study I did, through several teachers, through all of the John Thompson books. Finally, the teachers told my mother to find another for me so that I could advance more quickly. My mother listened.

I had come a long way since the first music recital, in which stage fright left a permanent scar in my memory.

"Try it again, Martha Sue." Mrs. Etheridge's words echoed from the back of the auditorium. I could hear her smiling, but I didn't dare look. Somewhere in the dark audience were my parents, my proud parents whom I had let down for the first time and I felt like all of Alabama was listening to the silence and saw my fear.

The words echoed again from the darkness at Robinson Springs School. When I sat down at the bench that night, suddenly I could not move. The paralyzing fear was one I would never forget. I bolted from the bench.

Though I would put behind me that first music recital, the silent apprehension would stay with me for life. Yet, I studied more. Soon I found that recitals were competitive. I remember looking forward to them after awhile, thinking I must be nearly the best since only one other student played after I did. How glad I was when Renee Owens graduated after my seventh-grade year.

Ardently, I practiced and studied music almost nonstop.

"Mama, I'd like to play the stereo," my brothers said. In the front living room was the cabinet piece in which the sounds of the Beatles cheered the neighborhood.

Daddy, too, needed space.

"Lois, make her practice 'nuther time. Shut the door," Daddy said. But it was not as though I could play outside. And I had to be really careful not to wake Daddy after he came in from a trip to Mobile. His hours were long, irregular, and unpredictable, and as children, all of us were expected to defer our daytime schedules to his.

My mother would never make me stop playing. Instead, she shut living room doors and told me to use the soft pedal, a habit I've never broken. She told me to play something quieter, and the damper created a muted sound I grew to like. In the recesses of quiet time, behind closed livingroom doors, I discovered Chopin and Mendelssohn. Mama had bought an entire music library from my grandmother's neighbor whose daughter had stopped studying music at the University of Alabama. I did not mark through Anne Ball's name written at the top of every book. I could not imagine anyone selling music. Maybe Anne didn't know.

Among the collection was Beethoven. I quickly discovered adagio movements and the "Moonlight Sonata." I found music that played. But it was not the music I studied with teachers. There was no play in the music I studied.

Etudes, Hannon's exercises, scales, Scarlatti. The only relief from the drill was the Schubert, which we dissected, memorized, eight measures at a time. The new music teacher, Mark McGowin, stopped me each time I tried to play.

He tapped rhythms with a short baton. He closed the piano lid and had me do finger and wrist exercises. First he demonstrated, and I stared at the nubbed fingers on his right hand. "Lawn mower many years ago," he explained before pressing on.

"Okay, one and five," he said as I lifted only my thumb and little finger and held them up to the count of four. Then he would try to catch me off guard. "Okay, now three and five." I worked on three and five quite a bit, even in school. I tapped out the calisthenics on my desk, hoping someone would notice my dexterity and ask me to explain.

I remember at first going to Wetumpka High School to study piano in the summertime with Mr. McGowin The school was closed, never any air conditioning until two decades later. Our 1960's model Bel Aire clouded the unpaved, red-dusty parking lot as we pulled up. Next door was the massive cotton mill for the working class, the teacher told me. He said Wetumpka was just a mill town with poor people who didn't know good music. I wondered what he thought of my working-class parents, of me, how I lived at the dead end of a dirt road. Did he know that? Why had he never mentioned anything about his close ties to Butler County, or other mill towns like those he first called home, Georgiana or McKenzie? Did he know my daddy could read only shaped notes?

I felt like an imposter, but I pressed on – because I knew I had to. After all, the music teachers before had told Mama I was not like the rest and she had listened. Everyone seemed to know more about me than I did.

I wanted to be the best, yet I wanted to be like the rest, as all children do. Somewhere in between, there I was. In the stifling August humidity, looking out a backroom-window at Wetumpka High School, I knew that very little separated me from the cotton mill next door, only the the dusty red-clay lot where no cars were parked in the summer, that and an old upright piano.

Mama took me to Wetumpka each week for a while. Then, Mr. McGowin left the mill town to teach at Stanhope Elmore High in Millbrook. At the height of the Civil Rights Movement and the first years of integrated schools, I was in another world, a safer world with my music, but at last, even that, someone seemed to own. That Mama helped create such diversions I'm now sure was no accident. Such worlds protected my sister and me from my father's tirades about moving to Australia to avoid the "new Civil War," even the Vietnam War to which my brothers certainly would be drafted.

And while the United States integrated its schools, fought the Vietnam War, and put men on the moon for the first time, I practiced finger exercises and tried to hold my wrists higher,

like the professional musicians did on public television. I watched
piano lessons broadcast from the University of Alabama.

Always, Mr. McGowin called me "Little Pal," never by name.
Scales and scales and arpeggios and keyboard exercises. To me,
they took away the music. Yet, I practiced them with fervor. There
was always a performance soon, recitals held by invitation in the
upstairs' studio of Mr. McGowin's home on Old Farm Road in
Montgomery. The house in McGhee Estates appeared a contem-
porary version of *Gone with the Wind*. Mark McGowin's wife was
a serious woman whose black hair was always tied back in a tight
bun. She watched and listened from the back with her arms folded. The room was filled with portraits of the Georgiana appanage.
Daddy said the family had money during the Depression, made
enough, in fact, to send Mark off to study music at a conservatory.
When he returned, he left Butler County, Alabama, moved from
the poor town of Georgiana to Montgomery. Now, gold-rimmed
mirrors reflected plush red carpet against white walls and ebony
stands with white marble surfaces. I marveled at the twin Baldwin
grand pianos in the center. Mr. McGowin and I played portions
of sonatas for two pianos. When we finished, we stood together
and bowed. Even that, we had practiced. Mrs. McGowin, like her
portrait, never said anything. Both cast a prudent eye toward the
piano. I felt like an imposter in this home of the Southern elite.
I just wasn't good enough. I was out of place: It just didn't seem
right that I should be here when I was simply the daughter of a
railroader who had been a high school dropout, and we lived so
far off the paved road.

At other times, there were recitals in the private home of
the Carters. Between Montgomery and Wetumpka, Jasmine Hill
was home to the elite. Their homes by the river bridged the gap
between the poor and those who could appreciate music, I supposed. I enjoyed the attention, the gardens with slate walkways

and running fountains, the cheese straws, punch, and the marvel of the rich. For a little while, I would be transformed from our home on the red-clay, Hickory Hill Road. Recitals among the privileged gave us an edge, we thought. We felt their admiration and envy. Humbled by poverty during the Depression, my parents grew proud.

"Money caint buy it," Daddy boasted.

Before age fourteen, I never minded performing, even on demand. I liked being the family miracle.

Soon, Mr. McGowin convinced my parents to plan to send me to a conservatory in Missouri. Quite likely the plan was simply one for purchasing music, but at the time, neither my parents nor I understood. At night, I lay awake, dreaming of the day I'd perform for hundreds, secretly fearful. Sometimes after school, when I might be in my room writing in my journal, I'd hear my mother on the phone, boasting of her plans to Hazel or Mary Campbell, tying up the party phone line. Mr. McGowin convinced us to sign a contract to purchase music from the conservatory, and I even got a silver ring with the school's emblem engraved on it. It was a silent pledge of my allegiance to music, my parent's contract with Missouri, and everyone's faith in Mark McGowin and me. Soon, music from St. Louis began to arrive. The brown packages with the St. Louis return label became symbols of the dream, a dream I soon began to fear. I was not ready for the conservatory, not ready, at age fourteen, to have my life after high school predestined. I did not want to be part of the plan, to be the centerpiece of my parents' living room. One day while practicing, I hurled the metronome across the living room, shattering it like Granny's China doll.

I turned inside, choosing to write and read more, unheard, masked behind the privacy of a closed door. In the silenced journals and hours of being transformed by Flaubert and Faulkner, I longed for my own voice. And I found it in the muted journals, or in the comic routines my sister and I played. With a simple queue from Gail, I could be the neighbor on the next hill, chastising her dogs, daughters, and husband; or the "library lady," pointing her finger at renegades congregating in the library before school ("Get out of MY library"); Gail's civics' teacher; or even Mama ("Yessir, Josephus," or "No, sir, Josephus," followed by a resigned sigh). I could be anyone except the prodigy Mama and Daddy expected me to be.

Before long, I rebelled, refused to play upon request, threatened to quit playing the piano – at least until my mother scouted for another teacher.

"You may stop, but you won't be able to quit," I remember Mr. McGowin predicted.

Mama researched until she found just the right teacher.

Gene Jarvis asked my mother to wait outside.

I remember the day I auditioned. Mr. Jarvis taught a limited number of students, so I felt the importance of the afternoon. Still, I had heard so much about the former Huntingdon College teacher that something inside me understood how life-altering this could be. My life and future were at stake. Besides, Mama was waiting in the car. She would not hear.

And when I sat down to play the soft Kawaii, I knew I had to reveal the poem inside me. I played Mendelssohn's "May Breezes" from *Songs Without Words*. I felt transformed. I played what I wanted to play, the music that reflected my soul, not the forced scales of Clementi and Kuhlau– necessary exercise, not music.

Something strange happened while I played: Mr. Jarvis did not interrupt me. There were no corrections during the piece. No one stopped me to say, "Try that again." He listened completely.

All Jarvis said when I finished playing was, "You really love music, don't you, Susie?"

And that was enough. It was good enough, and it was all I needed.

At last, someone understood. My four years of study with Jarvis were poetry. Debussey, Brahms, piano, harpsichord, the barely audible clavichord on a small Persian rug in an upstairs office. Bach, Mendelssohn, cherished new sounds on the massive, sacred organ at Memorial Presbyterian on South Court Street in Montgomery where the sanctuary was always cool. The sweet scent of the memory still brings back the wonder. I can still remember the pull of the massive gray double doors to the side entrance, the echo of walking across slate floors, waiting in the hall as another student's music reverberated.

For Gene Jarvis, I could deliver a concert performance, but when the church was filled, the mystique was somehow violated. My hands shook, my feet quivered, the notes revealed a nervousness unforgivable in the otherwise sacred setting. I much preferred the quiet of his home, his sensitive piano, his Persian cat Claude, a soothing, silent accessory to the mahogany piano.

I knew then, as did Gene Jarvis, that I was not destined for concert halls. Public performance was just too personal. The body was in the way. After my parents' push for the conservatory, outgrowing the gospel convention crowd that had propelled my first confidence, somewhere between the shyness of fourteen and the loneliness of music practice, sometime while I was writing in my journal and finding new voices – I knew.

That mine was the song without words, a silenced song, but mine, all the same. Still music.

Later I would know why I could not last as a performance major in college. The juries brought back the baton, the scales, the artificial music, and the insistence of too many music teachers all saying the same thing, "Try it again, Little Pal." Later, I would still think of myself as a failure, a disappointment to the parents who wanted to push me through a conservatory at fourteen. I would be too shy to even audition for college music scholarships. Never once did Gene Jarvis show disapproval

When Mr. Jarvis played, I imagined Bach himself in the music arched toward heaven. As the counterpoints resolved, I looked up at the stained glass window above the choir loft at Memorial Presbyterian Church on South Court Street in Montgomery, Alabama, a scene and a sound so permanently etched in my memory. Angled rays casting partial, bright four-o'clock sunlight seemed a testament, and I marveled at the revelation. Sometimes Mr. Jarvis would explain the Reformation, the commitment of musicians like Mendelssohn. And then I knew.

The glory of God, not me. Gene Jarvis had given me the tool to overcome my fear.

So many years later, I still repeat the lines as I play for church. And when I pray? I augment the introit – lead me, Lord. Lead me past myself.

Let me be an instrument, not the soloist. Thirty-three years later, I echo those words and remember Gene Jarvis.

Still, sometimes – especially when I play the piano as the offering is collected and I can hear money rattle, the focus drifts, I shake, miss notes I'd never miss. I am reminded of my inadequacy, of an audience, of feeling like the poor girl on display. Sometimes just hearing someone talk throws me completely off.

That is why so many years later it is okay not to have a concert hall or audience. I still prefer the sanctuary of the piano room, this in the home of the life I have built. It is a rich room of solace where comfort can be shared. Here, Plymouth-red walls contrast with proud white cotton in a crystal vase that tops the black Kawaii, the piano itself a high-school graduation present. Family pictures, an array of angels given each year by my piano students, my daughter's wedding portrait taken on the greens at Huntingdon College, my father's fifty-year-old felt hat from the Hub, some of his L&N Railroad records on the antique clipboard he used, stacks of music within easy reach, the antique maple library table Mama and Hazel found in an Autaugaville barn – these are the backdrop for Debussy and Chopin. My husband brings his favorite pillow, lies back with his arms folded. He asks for the *Nocturnes*; my daughters, the preludes.

Everyone prefers lying on the carpet to sitting in the Queen Anne chairs. Always, my daughters request the "Raindrops Prelude." When they were little, they would crawl up closely under the piano to listen for rain. And in the sanctuary of the piano room where there are no doors now, I know that it is okay. It is enough.

# XIII

## Good Enough for Daddy

My father's Hamilton  pocket watch was a token of his chronicles. Buying it  in 1941 was a prerequisite for working on the railroad so that the time he kept for the L&N could be measured accurately. The railroad had to run on time, he always said. I remember the watch,  the tales of how he'd had to save eighty dollars.

It was as old as his marriage, that watch. There was something almost mystical about its precision, about Daddy's preoccupation with the exactness of time and its ratio to money. Each railroader's watch had to be calibrated monthly and could not be off by more than a few seconds. In the yard office was the railroad clock, set each day by St. Louis time. The precision of switching trains to sideline tracks was exact. Railway cars had to be sidetracked to avoid collisions along the single-track lines.

The railroad depended on communication made through telegraphed or radioed messages announcing the next arrivals of trains. So time meant not only money, but potentially collisions. Flags posted too late could be disastrous. Daddy's sacramental care of the watch and the time that it kept thus were never questioned. We knew the importance of the railroad. We knew the critical importance of time.

Years later, Mother would joke about the watch. "Keeps time, but can't hold it." Daddy never laughed.

He would always caution about leaving for work early enough so that he would have time to change a flat tire along Highway 143, the highway  that followed the Alabama River, crossed it at the Tyler Goodwin Bridge to become Court Street. In fact, one could follow 143 all the way from Millbrook to the heart of Montgomery, the Court Square Fountain. There, one can look up the infamous Dexter Avenue and see the state capitol steps from which so much history has resonated.

Daddy followed the highway along its winding path to the L&N yard office, a lonely road at 3:00 a.m. in February, the car's headlights barely sufficient to light the way through the dark, suspended fog by the river. For as long as I could remember, Daddy drove a 1954 Ford to work. It had been tarnished by gray dust of the rail office. To get to the L&N yard office, Daddy passed beer joints along the Alabama River. Elmore had been a dry county, so the string of windowless joints along the way were establishments Daddy never patronized. He took pride in being a nondrinker, in the fact that he brought every paycheck home to his little wife and family. Hank Williams had sung at beer joints along the Montgomery Highway, but Daddy never heard him. A man like that, boasting about being all liquored up. And him from Butler County.

Daddy let nothing stop him along the way to the railroad office – not even the law.

He liked to tell about the time Millbrook's only law-enforcement at the time, the constable everyone called "Cowboy," stopped him at 2:00 a.m.

The story went something like this: "Cowboy," Daddy said, "I aint got time for playing games. They aint a soul out here but me and you and the road. Now, you just get right back in that vehicle and be on your way. I've got a job to do," Daddy instructed the constable who retreated, the story goes, and Daddy made it to work on time. He always did. He was never late and never missed a call. He chuckled each time he told the Cowboy tale. "Yeh, boy, I had a real job," he remembered. "No time for playin' cops and robbers."

Daddy kept time with the railroad. He chronicled meticulous records of time spent and money earned on the L&N. Often, men were called out to work on cold, rainy mornings, just as soon as they'd had their eight hours of sleep. Those eight hours, Daddy always told us, he and so many others worked hard for – every benefit was hard-earned by the unions. Daddy could relate the history of each strike, always named by the year in which it occurred. He told how union men formed picket lines until each basic right we know today was earned. Long before Social Security, long before the Wage and Hour Board, there was the railroad union, the brotherhood. Frequently, we were reminded of those ties and the sacrifices made.

As the family scribe, I have thirty-seven years of time books now, sealed away in clear plastic bags with zippers. Sometimes when the family is together again, we take out those old time books to see where Daddy was on a particular date. We note the gaps that show the Strike of 1953– or how much money Daddy made when inflation threatened the collapse of the economy, at least according to Daddy, a survivor of the Depression.

Michael has the Hamilton watch now, along with Daddy's five, ten, twenty-five, and fifty-year pens marking anniversary membership in the United Transportation Union. All are on display in untouched glass frames, sealed away from prying fingers of great-grandchildren who might be tempted to wind the watch that finally stopped. Mama was right.

Whenever the watch was broken or had to be calibrated, Mama would take Gail and me to downtown Montgomery. We took the watch to Rosen's on Court Street. The narrow store with its tall ceilings and creaking wooden floors was the Plymouth of turn-of-the-century business in downtown Montgomery, and carried some of its grandeur into the 1960's. Rosen's was just down from Montgomery Gun and Pawn where Daddy bought a pistol to protect himself from the Civil Rights Movement. I rarely went inside. Instead, I preferred to wait outside and study the iron bars on the windows. I wondered about the Iron Curtain and whether it looked like the bars on the gun store.

When we went down to Court Square to get Daddy's watch fixed Mama took me to Lee's Optical, because I'd had too many sick headaches. The sign said "one hour optical," but we waited longer than an hour. We went across the square to Belk's, where underwear was always on sale in bins in the middle of the store. Then we went to Kresses. We went in the front way, not the Monroe Street side. I liked the Monroe Street side better because that was the entrance for colored folk. And Gail and I loved to study the blacks. We looked adoringly at the babies and wanted so much to hold them. Once I even had Mama talked into letting me get a black baby doll from Kresses, but then she thought better. "Joe wouldn't like it," she said. I was keenly disappointed.

Instead, Gail and I talked Mama into always parking on the Monroe Street side. At least there we could observe the forbidden race. On the Monroe Street side was the soda fountain for the colored folk. We had to go upstairs to the mezzanine fountain, but when we did, we got a Coke and a doughnut, always the hallmark of a trip to town from Millbrook. Sometimes Mama let us wait upstairs at the fountain while she shopped. Gail and I spent hours peering over the mezzanine, observing the "Nigras" with their babies. Daddy didn't shop at Kresses. It wasn't good enough for Daddy.

When I got my first pair of eyeglasses, I looked all the way up the Square and saw tiny leaves on trees. I could see the sign advertising *The Sound of Music* was showing at the Paramount Theatre. When I looked up Dexter Avenue I could see the state capitol. It was as though a new world had been revealed and today was the first morning.

On the corner, we stopped by the Klein's clock and peered

into the jewelry store, or we would cross over to Montgomery Fair where white gloves were kept under glass counters. Sometimes we would go down to the fountain at Court Square, throw in pennies, and make a wish.

Across Court Square and the fountain was the Montgomery Hub, where Daddy purchased his clothes. The neatly pinned white shirts, gray or brown Crickateer suits and thin dress ties – all Daddy picked out for himself because he had to wear the best, and only the Hub was good enough for Daddy. Mama laughed about that.

What we didn't know in our early years we found out many years later. We learned, through extended family, about the pain of poverty Daddy's family had suffered not just during the Depression, but even before. Daddy never talked about his father much. All he said was that he got mighty liquored up and that the family lived on his Grandpa Lee's farm in Avant, timbering pines near Chapman to make a living. All that my father said about his own father, my grandfather Lee whose first name was never mentioned, was that he spent every dime on moonshine, so Daddy's own immediate family had little way to survive. Liquor, the lost farm and timberland, all were a shadow of my grandfather's destiny. The three-room dogtrot Daddy's family lived in was on the farm that failed during the Depression or before. Daddy's father lost the farm and the timber and the little bit of hope any might have mustered to live on during the Depression. Daddy sometimes joked that folks in Butler County never knew when the Depression hit because they'd always been poor. Nevertheless, the family lost the little they had, the lands that had been pioneered by ancestors a few generations before. Now, somewhere near Pigeon Creek, in an area hidden in the bottomlands, inaccessible by road, I've heard my father's grandparents are buried near the timberland farm that fell to the bank or Union Camp. How often I've thought about those mysterious graves out in the woods near Chapman. There, my great grandparents are buried almost anonymously, a fitting destiny of my father's unclaimed heritage.

As stories of the past go, Daddy's father had died as a young man. Moonshine got him. And Daddy, the oldest, became responsible at age fifteen. There is a cold and distant past unknown to many, buried in the hearts of those humbled by poverty so early in life. Poverty, that silent equalizer, was rarely discussed, but just a few years back, a surviving aunt told me the story. Students who could not pay their fees, which Daddy called tuition, were singled out at Georgiana High School, as they were perhaps everywhere. And so, just a few weeks into his tenth-grade year, to keep from hearing his name called out again for not paying fees, Daddy quit school. He traveled to South Florida to work on his uncle's farm by Lake Okeechobee. Later, he would drive a truck, carrying fresh produce as far away as New York City and Chicago. All so that he could support his family back home and put his sisters and brothers through high school. He liked to tell about buying their high school rings.

When he was home, Big Mama, Caddie Higdon Lee, would insist that Daddy's siblings give him the seat at the head of the table. In later years, Mama would say he still thought he was king, but she didn't treat him like one, and he wasn't her king. She said it was Jack, Daddy's baby brother by seventeen years, who was her hero. He had been a victim of polio early in life, sent to a children's hospital in South Carolina for three years. How often I have wondered about his survival and my grandmother's difficulty in choosing to put her youngest son alone on a train bound for territory she would never see. She didn't even drive, and besides, few had automobiles yet. Surely she must have wondered if she would ever see him alive again. But Jack did return, "all crippled up," Daddy said. Daddy said he couldn't work like other men, but Mama said he used his brains. And though he couldn't stand up straight, she said he was much more of a man than many she knew.

He had to order special shoes. One leg was longer than the other.

In later years we learned Daddy stopped in at the children's hospital to see Jack when he could. In fact, he planned his trips hauling produce from South Florida to the North so that he could see his little brother. Later his younger brother Fred joined Daddy in the trucking business. Together they visited their younger brother.

Never once, though, did I hear Daddy, Fred, or Jack talk about those visits or how Jack must have felt spending much of his early childhood hospitalized for polio. That's one of those things families don't talk about, the pain hidden between generations and siblings.

"Mighty right," I can almost hear my father say.

And though physically impaired for life, Jack never used the term "handicapped." He went to college and bought his own trucking company.

Mama sewed clothes for Gail and me and dressed us like twins because we were so close in size and not too far in age. We weren't twins, though. When you look back at the pictures, we look alike, except Gail is blond and I am brunette. The tiny little collars on the homemade dresses tell the story, the uneven collars, the pinched buttonholes where the buttons are too big, and Gail smiling because she has to. Daddy always liked that picture of Gail and me. That sparkle in my eye? I guess it always showed that I was Daddy's girl. But when you're four or five years old, you just don't know enough yet to look sad in pictures.

Mama had to dress good enough for Daddy. Sometimes I can still see my mother getting dressed for an all-day Sunday singing. Always slim, her high cheek bones the testament of Indian heritage, she reminds me of a movie star, and I wish I were that pretty. But Daddy says her skirt is too big, or she needs earrings, or her lips lack color, or she needs more rouge. And so she has to get dressed again, put on more lipstick and bigger earrings to be good enough for Daddy. He calls her his fine little woman. She just says, "Yes, sir, Josephus."

And I think, I think I will never be enslaved and will be good enough.

The newspaper clips showing the baby born with two teeth gave me an instant birthright of sorts, and gave Mama and Daddy bragging rights. And since age five, I had been playing the piano with both hands, Daddy liked to boast. Daddy called me his fine little chap, something I now see as enigmatic. I had been chosen, deemed good enough for Daddy. Of course, any child is happy to be accepted, though in retrospect it is easy to understand the discord among siblings, each trying to prove himself worthy of a parent's attention.

But just as I'd been born with two teeth and an uncanny musical ability – both of which I could take no credit for accomplishing – Gail and I had also inherited something else.

Guilt.

Mama always told her daughters far more than we wanted to know or hear. From early childhood, Gail and I heard about the sacrificial deliveries Mama made, how the doctors had warned her not to have any more children after Wayne's birth ten years before Gail's, yet she had done so just to have Gail and me. Despite the warnings, in spite of the doctor's advice, we had been born, not uneventfully: We marked two breech births. Gail and I had been delivered feet first, like cattle. The sacrifices were incomprehensible. Thus bearing the yoke of original guilt, we always listened to Mama. On one of those numerous occasions in which she would try to make sense of her life by explaining it to me, she told me how much she had wanted her first child, Michael.

She'd had Michael because she wanted someone to love, someone to love her. But Daddy? Daddy, she said, was actually jealous of the baby, of the time she took caring for him. He cried and cried, Mama said. Michael cried when he ate. He cried to go to sleep. He cried for someone to hold him, but the doctors said not to pick him up or he'd be spoiled. Mama regretted not holding the baby. She wished she had listened to her instincts, but she had followed the advice of the era. She threw up her hands. "Doctor knows best," she said. So many years later when Michael's appendix ruptured, the doctors learned his intestines had grown together in a jumbled mass. Mama's heart ached and never found resolve. She bore the pain of generations, never forgiving herself for any slight of decision or thought. Regret was never enough. Neither the Bible and salvation nor the devotion of her daughters and friends could bring consolation or peace. Gail and I laughingly called her Martyr rather than Mama, but there was nothing to laugh about. We had to find relief some way, Gail said.

"How do you spell relief?" we joked, echoing the Rolaid's commercials of the day.

Some relief came when Daddy traveled to Mobile several days each week. Whenever he was home, he slept in the daytime. No company could come when Daddy was sleeping. The sound of television playing, light switches clicking on and off, party-line telephones ringing, or Chihuahuas yapping uncontrollably with little provocation – anything could disturb Daddy's sleep. Everything we did in the course of a day would wake him. Naturally, as children we preferred those times when Daddy was in Mobile. Mama did, too. In fact, she watched the clock. Her clockwork depression was a fairly accurate gauge of when to expect Daddy home.

When he was gone, Mama could cook when and what she wanted, if she wanted, and take trips to Montgomery without telling anyone. When Daddy returned, he would check the odometer, always blaming the boys, in their teenage years, for excess miles put on the 1960 Chevrolet. Wayne broke the odometer, intentionally, of course, but made a joke out of it. Wayne could always make Daddy laugh. He was the Johnny Carson of the family, able to see humor even in Daddy's tirades about the check book. By then, Wayne himself had his own job and kept his own checkbook. He enjoyed picking on Mama about her indifference to accounting, but he must have known why she was so evasive about the exactitude of miles and money. It was the way she survived, her silent response to Daddy's control. Surely Wayne, who broke Daddy's odometer, understood.

Mama did what she knew how to do. Even as a child, I knew too much about family matters, like the household expense budget. She told me then, and she filled in the rest of the details repeatedly year after year, as though I didn't already know. Mama said she could stretch a dollar, but Gail and I observed that Mama could pretend. She was good at that. She could pretend money didn't matter, that Daddy couldn't own her. She did so by spending too much, often in secrecy. She didn't want Daddy to monitor her every move by knowing how every penny had been spent. To loosen the leash (her own expression), she just wrote checks without logging them, a practice she carried with her throughout life.

It must have been the ultimate revenge in the grave, so many years later, to have had the last word. The day Mama was taken to the morgue was the day I found out she had cashed her insurance. She had spent every last dime of her death benefit. The secret irony must have given her pleasure, time after time. She delighted in keeping secrets from Daddy, even those he could never know.

Michael was relentlessly dedicated to Daddy. Sometimes you could hear Daddy's voice in Michael's, but it wasn't one Daddy wanted to hear. So many years later, Michael would come to my rescue whenever Daddy faced surgery or hospitalization. He would serve guard in Intensive Care, ensuring that the careless actions of nurses on duty didn't jeopardize Daddy's well-being. Michael liked to tell of the near misses, how he'd intercepted the dosage that could have killed our father following Daddy's arterial surgery.

"They're trying to kill me," Daddy had cried, pleading for somebody – anybody – to just help me, help me, Lord Jesus. Michael always came, always listened.

Michael often would make the five-hour drive from his home in Florida to help, time after time staying long enough to get the torture and pain in abeyance, but Daddy was never grateful. Like clockwork, when the anesthesia had finally worn off and the pain subsided, Daddy would put Michael back in his place – his own words. He'd tell him to go home where his wife and children needed him.

Mama found Daddy's cruelty to Michael unbearable, unforgivable. I could never quite understand any of it. Whatever situation arose, we all seemed to do what we could to make sure that, whatever the circumstance, Daddy got the best treatment, that it was good enough for Daddy. He was treated like a king, only he wasn't Mama's king, and she didn't treat him like one. That job was left to Michael and me.

Gail? She could never take it, her own words. Ironically, at the time we thought she was the family member with the greatest dysfunction. We just thought she was selfish. But the longer I listen to my heart, the more I know now that everyone has to find his or her own way to survive.

Michael revered the man who could be so unnecessarily cruel to his oldest son. How much more did a son have to do to prove he was good enough for his father? Only the miles separated the silence of said and unsaid things as each child, now grown, found a way to survive.

Wayne moved thirteen hours away to Texas, where Daddy faithfully called him each Saturday, yet inexplicably he never called Michael. Mama would complain that her son in Florida didn't call her and that he didn't care. If she said anything about Daddy's weekly calls to Wayne, I don't recall.

Wayne's weekly recount of success in Dallas made Daddy proud. His boy had overcome the poverty that Daddy had known. He was prosperous. Wayne could make him laugh as he talked about the Arabs with all of their unsecured loans and oil money. But no matter how much money he made or how many yarns Wayne told Daddy, what was always left unsaid was that Wayne never felt good enough for Daddy. And through all my years of listening, I never knew the truth until so many years later. Only Mama knew. But as a woman often compromising to keep peace in the family, she said nothing – but heard everything.

The birth of a daughter brings total joy, devotion, unqualified love from a father; but a son often has to earn his place in the family and receives unwittingly a birthright of injustice.

Even through all of the joking, Daddy would warn Wayne to put away some money for a rainy day, stay away from alcohol, and to get himself back in church.

"It's not alcohol, Daddy – it's just beer," Wayne maintained.

"Caint lead to nothing but destruction," Daddy said. "I watched it ruin my father. Killed him." To Daddy, there really was no such thing as temperance – all alcohol, the first drink, one beer, a week away from church – all would lead to the same demise his own father had met drinking raw moonshine distilled in the Butler County bottomlands.

When Gail and I were children, every week we watched Wayne read the comic strips while we prepared for church or got ready for a singing, neither of which Wayne would attend. We were good little Baptist children, verbalizing our concerns and praying aloud for his salvation. Mama said not to worry because Wayne had been baptized before and that you couldn't lose your salvation. But Gail and I weren't so sure.

Wayne laughed and told all of us to mind our own business. He told us we shouldn't listen to everything we heard, and that one day we'd be able to think for ourselves.

Sometimes Daddy would just sniff and stay quiet in that odd way he showed disapproval. What Gail and I didn't know was that the quiet said more than we knew, the quiet from Daddy, from Wayne, and from Michael.

"Boy, you better put some'a that money away. Save it for a rainy day." Wayne was certain that Daddy just didn't know how to enjoy life. With the advice about money and liquor came another admonition: "Boy, you better give the Lord his due and be in church on Sunday mornings."

But Wayne had gotten as far away from Millbrook Baptist Church as he could, and he had no intention of turning back. Ever.

The rainy day did come when the Texas banks failed, and Daddy sniffed nervously without saying anything. If Wayne had told Daddy he'd indeed saved, that going back to school was feasible, Daddy wouldn't have listened.

All Daddy could see was the demise of his own father, the loss of the family farm, the future ruined.

And when Wayne's divorce came through, as though life weren't tough enough, once again the son felt the scorn of a father who'd been disillusioned.

Mama pleaded with Wayne to return to Alabama, to make a new start, but Daddy turned his head and sniffed in that nervous way he had. The unspoken "I told you so" could be heard, but Daddy spoke in the shorthand of his heritage.

"Curses, like chickens, come home to roost," Daddy said. "I guess all my children will be a disappointment."

Wayne was silent. It was the beginning of the growing distance that would never be resolved in Daddy's lifetime.

And so Wayne stayed in the wide open spaces of Texas and found freedom, not in the comforts of a family who loved him back home in Alabama. Instead, he left the big city life of Dallas and Fort Worth and turned instead to horses. For the first time, he found time for more than making money. That was something he didn't think Daddy would understand, and so the discussion never arose. Daddy would never understand the need for less, for less money, less obligation, less pressure.

When he moved from Dallas, Wayne swore he'd never be part of the race again, not the money race, not the competition for Daddy's approval – and Wayne needed none of it. The only race he wanted to ever take part in was a horse race. He never tried to explain himself to Daddy. Though he called weekly, it was a matter of ritual, and it was to Mama the youngest son preferred to talk, for she always listened and could read between the silences, as mothers do.

Daddy would never understand, so Wayne never told him. He kept silent. And distant. And he never talked about matters of the heart.

Not talking became the only way, the proven method of silenced retreat which allows a family to survive its own cold wars.

So many years later, Wayne wanted none of Daddy's heirlooms. The Hamilton watch, the railroad calendars, Daddy's wedding band, anniversary pins given by the Brotherhood – Wayne wanted no part in any of it. Michael kept the heirlooms, symbols, perhaps, of his uncanny ability to look beyond the father who was inherently, bitterly flawed.

Gail said we had a way of just seeing what we wanted, Michael and I, but each of us simply held on in his or her own way.

I know so much more now than then. All of us do. I can see that the distance Wayne placed between himself and Daddy was crucial, and perhaps more than anything else I can appreciate the brother who repeatedly bore the scoff of the man he most adored in life, his own father. In his own silence, Michael understood more than he acknowledged or anyone ever knew. And he adored Daddy in spite of it all. Like Jack, he was a silent, unsung hero who perhaps gave what he could not get, unconditional, unqualified love.

And the rest of us? We learned to keep quiet about what we could not bare to face, the hidden recesses of the man who so very much dominated the family that could never be good enough. Secretly, I chronicled the lives of those around me as I tried to understand. In so many ways, I was always the one to keep the family records. The sealed railroad time books I would one day see as a symbol of my role, but for the time, I was just listening.

# XIV

## Silent Bomb

When my parents placed me back in public school, I felt as though I were a character in one of the H.G. Wells' books I read at the time. Fumbling, silenced, fearful of the seemingly massive numbers of students, such a contrast from the four-room academy. So many years later, I still recall the first day, walking to my desk, certain that every eye noted my hair was curly, not straight like it ought to be, like everyone else's, that I was wearing an obviously home-sewn dress, green gingham with a matching hair bow. No one else had curly hair or home-sewn hair bows.

"If I keep silent, maybe no one will know I am here," I thought. My own voice echoed in my head. The practice of silence was one I soon mastered.

"She's awfully quiet," one teacher told Mama during open house. "Can't get much out of her."

I kept quiet for a long time, as long as I could. So when the news came at school that my mother had been taken by ambulance to the hospital, I felt almost as though I would explode, that I had no one to tell. If anyone had told me the year before that my mother's heart was broken, I would have agreed, but never suspected it would actually fail. But fail it did, that heart, again and again. So many times I'd heard Mama tell Hazel about her rheumatic heart, but then Hazel had been born with a hole in her heart and still lived, so, as children do, I didn't think too much about anything. But Mama's heart did fail. Maybe the doctors had been right. The last two children had been too much strain.

Still, I kept quiet. I kept quiet because I had to, because when you're a teenager, the world is your world and everybody should know that. I didn't know it then. I knew nothing of what I know now, only that my heart ached for unknown reasons. Why should my heart ache? It was Mama's heart that was failing. But in a way I knew nothing about, mine too was failing.

In the silence and darkness of the closet, I hid because the shadows of my heart told me it too would burst. And so I hid, I hid in the closet, hid for a long time. From what, I was not sure. Yet I was afraid that if I came out, if I faced the living room where Mama's drama played out too often, where cigarettes burned in the ashtray, where even Granny's clock ticking on the mantel reminded me of the labors of that time, I would explode. Then there would be words and tears and Mama couldn't take that. She shouldn't have to. I would have told Gail, but even that was not enough.

Teenagers should come with labels – caution, combustible.

When I did not come out, I heard the faraway sound of my own voice screaming to be heard until it actually became sound. Mama rushed in, but I could not stop screaming.

"What, Susie? What is it? What's wrong?"

I could not say.

Mama did her duty, what she thought was the only right thing to do. She tried to pry from me what had happened to make me so unhappy. But I didn't have the words. She asked me what was wrong. I could not tell her. I did not know. I didn't have the words.

In the silence of the counselor's office, I looked blankly at the blue-gray abstract art and wondered what it was supposed to be. Maybe it was supposed to be nothing, just color. I didn't know and didn't ask. The counselor, old, gray and with skin almost as blue as the painting, tried to pry words from me, but they wouldn't come – and so I said nothing.

"Do you like school, Susie?" he asked.

I nodded.

"What do you like to do for fun?"

I shrugged my shoulders.

"Your mother tells me you play the piano. What do you like to play?"

I shrugged my shoulders again. This went on for several weeks until the counselor finally told Mama he couldn't get anything out of me. Daddy complained about the cost.

There were diversions from the silence as Mama's hospitalizations grew more frequent and more intense. It seemed I sat with her for years at the hospital. Years, even into adulthood, even decades later.

"You never talk to me anymore, Susie," Mama said. "Are you worried about me, about my heart? We're going to be fine. You're going to be fine," she tried to assuage me.

What I didn't say, couldn't say, didn't know but felt all the same was that Gail and I knew about the heart. We knew more about it than Mama understood. We knew that it was broken and we couldn't fix it. But in my high school years, I didn't have the words to say to fix things. Gail and I later understood, with humor, our yoke of original guilt. But when you're fourteen or sixteen or even eighteen, you don't have the words yet. And so I said nothing.

At the hospital, as I sat with my mother, comforting her, serving almost as her interpreter to the nurses and doctors and Daddy, I held her hand.

Daddy walked in and tried to ignore the monitors that pumped out the irregular rhythms of her failing heart.

"Tell me you love me, Lois," he sought her assurance.

Mama said nothing.

"Just say you love me," my father repeated. "Just say it." He was insistent, certain she would die. He just needed to know, to hear the words once before her death. But the words would not come, and I could not make them. "She needs to rest, Daddy," I said.

Finally, Mama coughed. "Get that shit ass out of here," she pleaded.

How glad I was that Mama didn't die that day.

I have the words now, but I didn't then, and in retrospect I know why. Some cold wars are just necessary for survival.

For the first time in my life I looked around and acknowledged that the people in my family were not happy people. I felt Mama's heart had failed because I had done something wrong, and I knew that Daddy had only made matters worse.

The days when Mama got out of the hospital Daddy would joke about supper. "I'll eat anything you want to fix, Little Woman." But he was not joking. and Gail and I didn't laugh.

I wanted to make Mama well, but most of all, I wanted her to be happy. I wanted Daddy to be kind to her. It was a silent burden I carried and could not verbalize, because in the mind of a child, or even an adult, it's not our place to fix parents. I can say this now, but couldn't say it then. I can say it because Gail, Wayne, Michael, and I survived the silent cold war, and our own children will one day tell their stories, too.

And that will be okay. Mama said time takes care of a lot of things. She was right, and my own children will know that too. Parents can't always be perfect, Mama said. They can't always be happy either. I can say that now, but not then. I can say that now because one day my own children will embrace the imperfections that have created their uniqueness. That's what Gail and I did. And in our silenced retreat, we survived.

The books I read, the hundreds of books, the hundreds of hours I practiced the piano, the hours I spent writing journals and poems and making little books to give to friends, those were outpourings of love and pain at the same time, things I had to give away or hide behind because I could not understand what was right in front of me. Our home was not like *Leave It to Beaver*. Gail laughed about that.

We laughed most of the time, the two of us, even though she told me I was stupid and fat and would never make it in college. The cartoons she drew, the jokes I made, the characters I mimicked – we did that for ourselves. Because a cartoon or a story, we could laugh about.

We even joked about how Mama always expected the worst and repeatedly asked us, "What's wrong?" Neither Gail nor I could answer. What I couldn't say was that Mama, you were wrong – not that you had made mistakes, but that I sensed, Gail sensed, knew, that something deep inside was broken and we could not fix it. I don't think I ever gave up trying.

I only knew about the heart, the rheumatic heart, Mama's heart, the sacrifices made, and the overwhelming burden of being responsible. How unfortunate for parents that so few years in the course of a lifetime impact a person as much as those early years at home. It's one of those great injustices of life.

The teenage years were a period of darkness when I envied Michael and Wayne and knew I'd never live long enough to be an adult, much less get away from home. That's what it felt like, but I never said so, never did because I thought that the second I admitted it would be the one in which I gave in, and there were times. The words don't hurt as much now as they did then. Now I am a parent and a teacher who can and does try to look adolescents in the heart and hear it breaking and try to convince them that though the days seem forever, one day they'll understand – if they can just wait.

Words don't create reality by being spoken or appearing on a page, but somewhere in all of this, I hope to give others the courage it takes to survive fear. And they will be free. That's what I'll tell them. But when you're a teenager, just trying to survive is an effort in itself, one that can't be verbalized.

Mama and Daddy spent a great deal of money financing my musical education, Daddy always reminded me. Those many hours weren't really wasted. Behind closed doors was the only place I could be a star, and I always knew my parents were listening, though that wasn't enough at the time.

Gail and I had our individual ways of surviving. Everyone did.

In the silence of unspoken hearts, everyone is afraid that another will fire the first truth, so no one says anything. To do so would complete the disintegration of the family, cause complete, final, irreversible destruction

Even now, Gail, Michael, Wayne, and I all share the shadows of those silent years. But that's how you survive a cold war.

# XV

## Bears

It was fall in the decade of the 1970's, the Age of Aquarius, a period I would later understand to be a turning point. I was almost seventeen, just like the magazine I read in the library before school each day. Man had walked on the moon, and times were changing.

When Gail went to college, for the first time I was truly alone. I could almost hear Hazel tell me I could go to school in two years, could feel that silent  hunger inside pleading, "now, now." Youth is not a time for patience. The peace rallies of the 1960's had done nothing for me.

Alice Cooper reigned, along with Led Zepplin and the Almond Brothers. Our banner song? – "School's Out Forever."

Outside, the wind whispered promises through the hickory trees– my birthday was coming up the next week. But I couldn't have a birthday without Gail. It wouldn't be the same. Without Gail, I had no desire to listen to Alice Cooper or even the Doobie Brothers. When I played the piano, it seemed no one was listening, and for the first time that mattered.

Wherever I went I could feel the silence. Gail wasn't there. And to me it seemed she never would be back, never in the same way we had known growing up in the woods where the red-clay road held our secrets and promises.

Alone, and no need to have Gail second every decision I made or remind me that my eyebrows were growing together and that curly hair wasn't really cool. There  would be no one to straighten my hair with Curl Free the night before school pictures or reassure me that I really didn't look too much like Cleopatra with such very coarse, straight hair– straight at least one day of the year.

Alone, and there was no space for our daily dialogue to temper Mama's sadness and Daddy's demands with our own brand of humor. In me, Gail found the comedian who could play out Mama's and Daddy's act with subtle satire and voice and sighs. "Yes, sir, Josephus." "Yes, sir, whatever you say, sir." I wondered so many times why Mama didn't turn around, smack Daddy, and just for once say, "By God, no. I'm tired. You do it yourself, Joe." Or just sweetly, kindly, serenely, say just for once, "Go to hell, Joe. Go to hell and don't come back."

I could mimic every teacher in school, even the library lady, as we called her, who each day demanded that the rough, loud guys get out of her library. Or I might be the lady on the hill above our house, chastising her dog Fritz to "git off this porch," or yodeling for her husband to come back from the garden. "Howwww-wwwweeeerrrrd! Time for supper!" You could hear everything in the hills. We joked that the neighbors in the valley below our hill could hear Daddy clear his throat, fart, or call, "Ooohhhh, Lois – your little dog has done her job again."

But alone, the jokes were gone, and I had no audience, no co-conspirator, no ally in our defenses against Mama and Daddy's depressing dependency.

There were many things I knew I could not fix, Mama and Daddy, primarily, but the broken relationship, the overwhelming unhappiness inside the home could not be avoided. Going outside just didn't seem to help. Mama was anxious about Gail's first year in college, and her own happiness, and mine, were not priority. As was my custom by then, I said nothing.

Mama said the fall was a sad time of year, a time of loss when shedding leaves predicted a cold, rainy winter and an early frost.

Years past, I could remember getting off the school bus, how the dogs would circle and wag their tails, each day a sort of routine reunion. For me, fall meant change was promised. It held the excitement of something new. I would see blue sky overhead as though for the first time, and like the moon, it always seemed to hint more than I could even say in a poem. And I wrote poems, which I kept in journals and shared only with my closest friends, like Carol, who didn't criticize me like Gail did. I never would have shown Gail my poems. Carol told me that I was talented, and we went to church together. Gail didn't go, never wanted to. I wanted her to hear me play there in the sanctuary of the church, but she said she heard me every day. I never bothered to explain.

How could anyone understand why I missed her so much?

I wondered where Gail was at the very moment I thought about her, imagined that we could be sisters in college and not have to answer to Mama or Daddy or anybody. It wasn't fair that she should be free while I was still trapped in her shadow. It didn't seem fair, because I had always been bigger. And just when did she become the leader?

The scent of her hair spray and Bonnie Bell nail polish still filled the back of the house, and I could almost hear Carley Simon in the room next to my own. But the room next to my own was empty now. Even Chee Chee Pooh found no comfort in sleeping on Gail's bed.

The car was all mine to use, but without Gail, I wondered for the first time where we used to go. When the phone didn't ring, the solitude was very personal. And I knew our lives would never be the same, that something inside had changed forever in a way that only sisters could understand.

In the early 1970's, at least at our house, long-distance calling was taboo. Besides, there were no phones in Gail's dorm room. In fact, each hall had only one phone.

What could I have said? I'm sorry, Gail. Come home. Don't leave me here to keep Mama and Daddy together, because I can't do it. Chee Chee Pooh misses you, and so do I. She would have laughed at that point, and so would I – because it covered up what I really meant to say but never could, still can't –- that, Gail – you're my sister, my soul, the kindred laugh that knows the punch line before it's told, my best friend, no matter what. We are like question and answer. Where you go, I go. Where one leads, the other follows.

That we were Girl Scouts together, so many years – sisters. A Girl Scout is a friend to all, and a sister to every other Girl Scout. Remember? Troop 75. Girl Scout Law Number Four.

But I couldn't.

Mama said that if everything went well, and if I didn't get tonsillitis again, I could go see Gail and maybe stay the weekend. Driving down the highway I felt free – I was going to see Gail. I was nearly seventeen and the road was mine. Beyond the radio and the windows rolled down, Daddy's warnings about alcohol and strangers seemed a lifetime away. He wasn't really talking about me, I knew. What was there to fear?

As I drove up to the dorm, I looked to the trees, because I always look to trees, evaluate their age almost immediately and strangely assess how to negotiate a climb. Tall trees, planted oaks, magnolias almost as tall, and in full white bloom even in October.

As I signed in and waited for Gail to retrieve me from the oversized, tiled parlor, I noted how institutional the place felt, with its cracked, black sofas and unfriendly "dorm mom." She was like a nurse who wouldn't hesitate to give you a shot right in the butt without warning. I could almost smell rubbing alcohol, and I wondered why Gail liked this place better than home. On the wall were listed so many rules. There were shared bathrooms, no privacy. How did Gail find such a place freeing?

We walked all over the campus and Gail showed me the theater building where she designed sets. We walked to the dining hall, and all along the way guys waved at Gail as she excitedly motioned, "Hey, this is my little sister!" I tried to conceal my breasts and longed to be petite like Gail.

And so that weekend I tried not to mention anything about home or Mama and Daddy, because I knew Gail liked school and wouldn't come back if I said too much. Parties? Sure. I didn't dare mention I'd never, ever been to one and didn't really want to go. But somewhere along the way I had become the follower, silenced by her older sister. Just when that happened for sure, I couldn't tell.

I wanted to tell her that Mama makes me sad and that she wanted to leave, but Gail wouldn't understand that either, so I kept my mouth shut. Gail never understood about Mama then.

Rita Coolidge's voice filled the second-floor dorm and spilled outside the dorm room as we waited for night there with Gail and her friends. There was no air conditioning, and the windows opened in sheer testimony of Gail's new freedom.

"One day I'll be a concert musician. Even Gail will have to listen. And she'll say, 'That's my little sister,'" I thought.

Gail's friends were not the kind who wanted to hear about what I did back in Millbrook. Here there was fun, you know, like fun – you girls want to have a good time? But Gail was gone and I didn't know – everything seemed okay, I mean the guys didn't even have acne, but nothing was really right.

When I had thrown up the first beers I'd ever had, I knew that it had come in the middle of my pleading, "Stop, stop." In the darkness of near unconsciousness came the warning to flee, run for dear life. But I couldn't.

Stop, stop, I was afraid, I was asleep, I didn't know, I didn't know that this was supposed to be fun, because it wasn't, and when I came to I was hitting, hitting hard and crying and saying stop, take me home, take me home, and I hurt and my head spun around and I couldn't find Gail. Take me back.

I couldn't click my heels and go back to where I had been less than twenty-four hours before. Something about my life had changed forever. I wanted to forget, but even through the confusion of inebriation was a clear awareness that all had gone very, very wrong.

What would Mama say? It was my fault, because I didn't have to drink, should have known better than to be alone with drinking guys. Somewhere in my memory Mama had said guys would "take advantage" of girls who drank, so it was my fault – I wouldn't tell. Couldn't. Mama would blame Gail and want to know where she was. It wasn't Gail's fault, Mama. She didn't know anything would happen.

She is my sister, my best friend, and I'm her little sister. A Girl Scout is loyal. So I couldn't tell. A Girl Scout is clean in thought, word, and deed. From that day on, I would have to be anonymous. I would draw more into myself to hide from the world outside, because the outside world was a dark place to be, darker than inside myself. And I had learned. I had gone far from the shield of Hickory Hill, and it would take me many years to get back. Until then I would have to be quiet.

Gail was right. She was right about college not being the place for me.    And something else.

She was right about the bears.

# XVI

## Mama's Turn

Everyone has those moments in life that mark the day or time of great change. My turning eighteen was one such epiphany, not so much for me as for my mother. She could be free at last. And I could set her free. It was a heady responsibility, and it seemed like the right the thing to do. Mama had thought about this for a while, and, truthfully, so had I. Never would I have imagined, however, that she would involve me as a co-conspirator. Nevertheless, the time had finally come. Mama had finally decided to take action to regain her life – she could be free at last. And in a strange way, I felt that freeing her would also free me, from what, I wasn't sure. But after the silent episode at Gail's college, I had withdrawn into a world of writing and music, away from the world, away from everyone. I too needed a change and had to fight the urge to just run.

While my friends talked about high school graduation, boyfriends, what they wanted to be or do, how they couldn't make up their minds – my thoughts were turned to other matters centered around the needs of Mama. Daddy was already worried about what my going away to college would do to her. He said she wouldn't know what to do, but I secretly knew Mama grasped exactly what to do. She was planning her own getaway. For good. Looking back I think it was Daddy who was most afraid of my going away to school. Likely, he knew that sending his youngest child off to college would also mean the dissolution of his marriage, but I didn't think about all that at the time. Through everything that was either said or unsaid, the feeling from all around was that I seemed to owe something to my parents that I could give neither. Looking back, I see that what I felt was in some ways just more of the original guilt Gail and I had inherited at birth, but I didn't know it at the time. Neither did Daddy.

Before I could graduate, Mama made plans. I couldn't tell my sister Gail or anyone. I had just turned eighteen when Mama verbalized her dream about leaving. She wasn't referring to my future college plans – she was going to leave Daddy.

"I've stayed for you girls," she told only me. By then Gail was a sophomore. Mama's job was done. "Now I need to leave, leave this place, leave Joe. Can you understand that?" she asked, waiting for my consent.

"Sure, Mama," was all I could say. I didn't have the heart to tell her I wanted out too.

My job, I soon learned, would be to help carry out her mission in total secrecy. I was thrilled to take part in something so surreptitious. I made the promise. And when I did, I promised also to free myself, to leave when I could, just where I wasn't sure. All I knew was that there was a gnawing fear inside, a fear that had only grown since the episode at Gail's school, and I had no answers for it. I'd rather she left now than be disappointed when I couldn't make it in college, and I sensed that too was coming.

"Can you forgive me?" she asked repeatedly. If I had been more mature, I would have asked her the same question, but the silence inside me wouldn't answer. Besides, forgive her for what? It was a question I didn't quite understand. All our lives, Gail and I had wanted her to be happy. She had lived her whole life for others, for me, for Gail, for our brothers, for our father. When the railroad phoned my father to work before daybreak or just as we sat down to a holiday meal, Mama responded. Without question she would silently scramble an egg, fry chicken, burn cheese toast, pack Daddy's lunch, and brew coffee. And for many years, when we had only one car, Mama would take Daddy to work, even at three a.m. Gail and I slept in the back seat as Mama drove Daddy to the yard office.

At other times we'd leave late at night to pick Daddy up. We hoped to see engines turned around noisily in the Roundhouse that stood in the middle of the dusty-gray rail yard. Men unloaded their baggage from the red caboose, their railroad lanterns always in hand. I wanted to ride the caboose where the men ate and slept – it seemed like such adventure. Instead, we waited and watched.

All of us spent a lot of time waiting and watching. I listened and observed. I watched as my mother never sat down, even to eat, until she collapsed to watch the ten o'clock news. She lived in a state of waiting. I remember thinking how sad and silent she seemed as she stood there ironing, and I wished so many times Alice had not left. She was such a help, such a friend to Mama.

"Lord, just get me through the day; a better day's a'comin'," Mama would sigh. Sometimes, she'd hum the hymn "Others." In the background were the melancholy sounds of familiar soap operas. I learned to play the organ music from memory as Gail and I played out our daily exposure to *Days of Our Lives* or *Another World*. We talked about the character Patricia – who even now seems like a cousin unseen since childhood, but whose presence in the early years was so clear.

Maybe at last there would be no more waiting: the time had come. So secretly I was elated. Forgive her for what?

"Don't be silly, Mama. We'll be fine. I just want you to be happy. But why can't I tell Gail?" I asked.

"She can't keep a secret," Mama said. But I knew she could. She and I had made a lifetime practice of keeping secrets. Still, I said nothing.

Mama stashed away cash and packed her bags, but beyond leaving, she really had no plan. The decision to leave was enough. I felt special to be part of the conspiracy that would bring an end to the waiting. I did not want to carry the burden of Mama's sadness any longer.

And on the appointed day, we carried out our mission. I drove her to the Trailways Bus Station in downtown Montgomery where she bought a bus ticket to get out of Alabama. She wouldn't tell me where she was going. It didn't matter, I assured her. "You'll be okay," I promised. Looking back, I can appreciate the irony of her departure. When she should have been seeing me off to college, instead I was setting her free. But nothing of those thoughts entered my mind at the time. My purpose was singular – let Mama go. I'm grown up now, and she'll be fine on her own. It was a day of freedom for both of us.

At that moment there were no tears. There was no time to doubt the decision that had been made by either of us. Finally, I had been able to do something positive for my mother. Although I didn't understand then, I do now; she trusted me to understand her, to recognize that she was a person, too – not just a mother and wife, the one who always cooked, but never sat down even to eat.

And so on that clear autumn day in 1973, I left my mother at the bus station without looking back. All the way home from downtown Montgomery to Hickory Hill Road, I sang along with the radio. As I soloed the car across the Tyler Goodwin Bridge, I knew Elton John was right– the highway did look sweet and free. And freeing my mother had set me free.

"Confound the luck. You did what?" Daddy asked. Gail was home from college, and to my surprise, she was equally outraged.

"I took her to the bus station. She just wanted to go. I just wanted her to be happy," I rationalized. Until the confrontation, I had felt heroic. No one knew anything until Mama had had hours to get away. Suddenly, my joy was deflated.

"Susie, I can't believe you would just take her to the bus station. Didn't you think at all?" asked Gail. I couldn't believe her words. Didn't she know? Was this really my sister asking these questions?

A heaviness unlike anything I'd ever experienced filled the house. Daddy said nothing. Instead, he sniffed nervously and peered sideways as though looking for an answer. From time to time, Gail would repeat, "Susie, I just can't believe you did it. Didn't you think of the consequences?"

I was speechless.

There were no words for the feelings I had, the overwhelming need to make Mama happy. It never really occurred to me that doing so would make me a villain, and I thought certainly Gail would understand. She didn't.

Gail phoned Wayne and Michael. Soon everyone seemed to know. The phone rang constantly, echoing a nervous tension that no one could break. With each ring came the hope that this time it would be Mama. Instead it was Aunt Ruth or someone from the church following up on the "prayer chain."

"Susie, have ya'll heard anything from Lois?"

"No, we haven't heard a thing," I would say. As the culprit, I always answered the phone. It was a measure of atonement.

"We're praying for all of ya'll, and if you need anything, you just call. Such a shame– poor li'l Lois– you know she's got that bad heart and her health aint good."

No one could believe what I had done. I told Daddy I was sorry. What I didn't say was that I was only sorry for him, sorry that he felt so lost and broken. Inwardly, I still applauded Mama. In my silence I prayed that she would keep going and that she would get very, very far away. I remembered the vows I had made to Mama, the excitement we shared as she planned to leave, my promise to set her free and stand behind her. And so the retreat to my room was one of singular joy. As Gail and Daddy made frantic phone calls, I read or wrote in my journal. The three weeks that passed seemed like months. When the runaway finally called, she talked to Gail first. She said she was working as a waitress in Pensacola.

Her feet had swollen. Then it was my turn.

"I hate to do this to you girls," she told me. "Can you forgive me?" Mama's voice sounded tired, faraway, desperate.

"Do what, Mama?" I said with unspoken disappointment. How could I possibly tell her that I didn't want her to come home? The words would not have come out right, and so I kept quiet.

Still I pleaded with Daddy and Gail. " Leave her alone. Let'er go. Mama'll be all right."

"She aint all right," Daddy said. "Poor li'l woman caint make it workin' – she's give out."

Daddy and Gail would not listen, and so they left, determined to rescue Mama in Pensacola. I stayed home, read *Crime and Punishment,* and hummed along with Rita Coolidge and Carley Simon. At least they understood.

I made a new promise, this one to myself.

Nancy Friday wrote in *My Mother, My Self* that three life events turn us into our mothers: getting married, becoming a mother ourselves, and losing our mothers. I vowed to break the pattern, the mold, to prove Nancy Friday wrong. Never would I be dependent. Never would I think someone else held the power to make me happy or miserable. Never would anyone force me to do anything I didn't want to do. Never would I sacrifice my self-identity and interests for the sake of a man or even children. I would spend my life proving that I was not like my mother if I had to. In my diary I wrote the truth and made the new secret promises. And I told my diary Gail was wrong about Mama. So was Daddy.

From that day on, I knew the quest for that elusive sense of freedom had begun, and I never gave up trying to free Mama. After all, I promised.

# XVII

## My Turn

From the clouds of teenage years, so far beyond them now, I look down to see a young girl with a pen, writing. She writes that one day she too will get out, just like the girls in her books, and that she will look far beyond this time now and it will be small. Sometimes she plays the piano alone, the damper secured, the doors always shut. From the solitude of Chopin and Mendelssohn come the songs without words, waiting to appear.

"What? What do you need? Words? More paper?" I ask. She cannot hear me yet, though something inside her tells her to listen. In the distance, a train sounds.

So many years later, my husband, Dwan, tells me that about the time I was learning how to write in cursive, he was sitting on the back of an airplane, thousands of miles away from home. As he gazed into the stark sunset over Thailand, he wondered what time it was in Alabama. Most of all, at age nineteen, he just wondered, "What the hell is communism?"

So many times he thought that at that very moment he ledged upon a point of no return. If anyone had said, "You can go home, Boy; you'll just have to walk," he would have taken off right then, on foot. It would not have mattered. Often he has wished he had just met me years sooner. But that could not have happened, not at least before my chrysalis. We were still worlds and wars apart.

Gail had been right about college. After one semester away from home, after the remarks of a piano teacher advising me to go home and look at the sky awhile, I left the University of Alabama, the same school where a decade earlier George Wallace had vowed "segregation forever." Going home was a regrettable decision. There would be more.

In the fog of my memory the months seemed like years, the uncertainty of school, changing schools, trying to decide whether to even attend or not, the indecision about changing my major. I was supposed to be a musician. What could I possibly do if I weren't playing the piano or organ or attending a master class where so many had curly hair and bobbed their heads collectively as the music played? All my life I had been a musician. Even if I did decide to continue music in Montgomery, where could I study? The private Methodist college, Huntingdon, was out of the question, far too expensive for Daddy, who was ready to retire. Looking back, I can understand the dilemma we both faced, Daddy, old enough to be my grandfather, and I. Before that time I never appreciated the generation gap, and for the first time in my life, it became apparent. My parents were old enough to be my grandparents.

Struggling to hold onto a dream I knew deep inside was unattainable, I did the unthinkable: For a few short weeks, I was enrolled in an all-black Alabama school. There I was truthfully studied as the only white girl on campus. Even though traditionally all-white schools had become thoroughly integrated by that time, white students had not yet crossed over to attend all-black schools. Though I lacked the courage to be one of the first, I wanted to try because at the Montgomery college, I could study music with some of the best-known musicians around and perhaps keep the dream alive. And if not for my own insecurity about being the only white girl, I felt a more relaxed acceptance than I had felt at the University of Alabama. But I could not relax because the stares were culpable. This school was not a white university, and although I would be tolerated, I would not be accepted. In my heart, I wanted to stay – not only for the music, but perhaps to silently avenge my father's prejudice.

With my Indian-dark skin and dark, curly hair, I could perplex a few students. The Afro was natural. One student came right up to me, stopped to peer right into my face, and asked me quite frankly if I were black. I was stunned.

She studied me, then turned, having satisfied her own question. "Yeah, you   black." And she walked away. The confusion brought silent satisfaction, but I could not blend in so well with the majority. Later I might reflect back upon what it really felt like to be a minority, but not then.

And so when my black classmates offered me warnings about where to park and to make sure that I was accompanied at night, something inside me said "run." Leave. I was getting pretty good at that.

Somewhere in the fog of my memory are bits and pieces of the ultimate decision to run, to leave, to escape the home and life in which I felt trapped. And so I left at night with a nineteen-year-old boy, really, one I'd dated for a year or more, off and on, but knew little about. It didn't matter. He said he read Tolstoy, so I believed. I never saw him read anything. He played steel guitars with amps but never finished a song. His car stereo incited the attention of neighbors and policemen, but it didn't matter. His mother said he wanted to be a writer, but he never wrote anything. He gave me his electric typewriter because he wasn't using it. And in the dead of night, after a few beers to muster up the courage, I packed my pillow and my journal and told Mama goodbye without looking back. Mama had returned from Pensacola, only to see me leave. Daddy was in Mobile, which made my job easier.

Retreat with honor. Peace. Nixon's promises didn't make the fall of Vietnam, or me, any easier. There would be fallout, for everyone.

I couldn't be Daddy's girl anymore.

# XVIII
## Revolutionary Zeal

There is a certain exegesis that looking back upon growing up affords those like me who survived ourselves long enough to appreciate the journey. And so we search for those explanations and allow memory to canopy the light and the dark together, to shade in those foggy areas that seemed to play no real part in the process of maturing, but offer some excuse for the quest, itself a departure.

I ran away without looking back, running from something I could not even define or acknowledge. Where I went seemed less important than just getting away, and harking back to that other time I can see that the distance I created between my parents and me in the following few years was a necessary though painful step. While my friends went to college, I simply went away.

Two weeks after the hasty departure, a gut feeling to run back home enveloped me. It was as though a part of me had died. Mama sent white flowers, an ornate arrangement that could have been placed equally beside the marriage altar or tombstone, and I was embarrassed. Although the desire to retreat was almost over-whelming, the equally gnawing question now was, "Where would I go?" I knew I could not go back home. You didn't do that in Joe Lee's house. There was no where to turn.

I could hear my father warn me that my poor li'l mama was mighty worried, but in my egocentric world, I rationalized it was they, Mama and Daddy, who couldn't understand. Rather than give in once again to the desire to run, I retreated into a world of writing, music, playing college. Although I had gotten only two hours away from home, the distance could have been measured in planets, it seemed. I made it all the way to the Peanut Capital of the World, Dothan, Alabama, where I could study Chaucer at a night school, play my music, read, and write all day. That's what I did. That I was now married hardly mattered.

I stayed married four years, but even now I can't even remember what that was like. Instead, in the cloud of my memory that may be a dream, I see the young girl who didn't mind that she had no means of transportation except by bike, who sold Coke bottles for cigarette money, who walked to the nearest church to have a piano to practice. In the solicitude of playing and writing and reading came a newfound freedom, the clarity of independence, albeit unfunded.

And along the way, I simply grew up. By the time I returned home for a visit, I found something unexpected had happened, more so in me and the way I viewed my family than in anything or anyone else.

Perhaps for the first time, I truly understood that while I had been a product of the 1960's where the banner was "the generation gap," between my father and me, there really existed such a disparity. He was old enough to be my grandfather, and as he aged and I grew up, it was suddenly very apparent. I would grow to appreciate the great divide as a protective gap.

My father had turned into an old man, a broken man, in many ways, a man who, like George Wallace, I now saw was to be pitied rather than feared. There was my father, by then sixty-seven years old, and I, his youngest daughter, only twenty years old. Only he wasn't Granddaddy; he was my father. Perhaps subconsciously at that point, I began to see him differently, as a man who was less formidable as a cranky old granddad instead of Daddy. Silently, unknowingly, somewhere along the way I began to view my parents not as my own but as grandparents. They were somehow less imposing that way, their influence far less daunting. For the first time I saw that I could be myself, not just their daughter. In the intellectual awakening all young people undergo, of course, I thought I was the only one who had ever experienced such feelings.

For the  first time, I could distinguish my own views from those of my father, and even though Mama had been trapped, I could see her choices as just that, her own choices, her decisions, not my responsibility. She did a balancing act, staying with Daddy, but for now, I was not in the circus. From the sidelines, I could watch, leave when I wanted, and understand a little more.

So I watched as my parents grew old, as their attitudes mellowed, as their circumference of influence diminished. As I began chronicling my observations, my awakening as a person coincided with the life of a young writer, and I knew that this had always been my role, but now I could use it to gain a better perspective not only of my family, but also the world into which they had borne four children. I had survived. It would be a lifetime later that I would realize each in the family had taken the steps needed for survival, each in his or her own way.

My father was a man of strong politics and principles, his own brand of dogmatic wisdom, I suppose. He always  sought the kind of politics and religion that would validate his biased tendencies. That he followed evangelists and politicians alike should have come as no surprise. Looking back, I can see now how the pieces fit together. My father was an emphatic man. When he retired from the L&N Railroad, Gail took him to hear Bob Ingram speak at Auburn University at Montgomery. How fitting that Daddy should align himself so closely with the quick-witted man who'd editorialized the Wallace Era for the *Montgomery Advertiser* and the local TV station. Daddy was so inspired that he talked about working on his GED and going on to college. Gail encouraged him; we both did. But Daddy chose instead to attend rallies and read *U.S. News and World Report* along with the Colliers yearbooks. He chronicled history back to World War I and was convinced the early Republicans caused the Great Depression. He was still certain that there would be another, which he predicted during the Nixon era.

And so I watched, now from the sidelines.

We had accompanied Daddy to rallies and speeches and singings all our lives. Somewhere in the folds of memory, I could remember being a twelve-year-old, sitting beside my father in a hot auditorium in August.

We were there to hear Billy James Hargis, just the kind of revolutionary evangelist my father could believe. On a sweaty summer day, the preacher with missionary zeal brought his paperback books and tapes to display to a crowd gathered to hear him in the sweltering auditorium of Robinson Springs School. Separation of church and state is a relatively new concept. Not so long ago, and still in many areas of the South, schools were community centers. At schools, gospel singings were held and missionaries met to spread the Word and plead for money. Billy James Hargis was a different kind of missionary. He was not trying to church the unsaved in any foreign land. His goal instead was to save us from the insidious moral decay of rock-and-roll – the drug culture. Why, Satan himself was right here at work in the United States of America. Communism threatened all around. Hargis pointed to evidence of communism in the lyrics of the Beatles' music. My father believed. He gave money. He bought books. He took home pamphlets. At the Admiral Semmes Hotel in Mobile, he shared them with politicians like Senator Jim Allen who frequented the lobby to garner support from railroad union men.

I remember the splintered wooden seats of the auditorium chairs, the round evangelist with the red face, his arms gesticulating the widespread threats all around us – they would break up homes, cause teenagers to experiment with LSD, incite sexual immorality through dancing and mini-skirts and a generation of teenagers who had no respect for authority. All of it was the infiltration of a communist plot.

Surely, somewhere in the mixed message there was a plea by the reverend for the nation to turn back to God, but I don't recall. The pieces of memory are puzzling; only an impression lingers. I remember thinking that there were so many people who understood much more than I did, because I could not make out anything communist in the lyrics of the Beatles.

But Daddy had mellowed somewhat as he grew older.

Integration, communism, LSD, the Beatles, liberals like George McGovern and Hubert Humphrey – one by one, the impacts of the threats Daddy had thought jeopardized the stability of his family did not vanish so much as they simply faded. Years later, when Daddy had grown much older, he lost some of his zeal. Instead, ironically, he found humor and reveled in the downfall of politicians and television evangelists. He verbalized his amazement that the "niggers in Alabama" could re-elect George C. Wallace. He said it proved two things – that Wallace was a politician and that "niggers" would buy into anything. Then he would laugh. No more were the political threats in Alabama a real danger. Later, he would enjoy just as much fun when the governor/evangelist Guy Hunt, an Amway and vacuum cleaner salesman, could con Alabama voters into supporting his political ministry.

And little by little, as he quit going to church and instead watched television, he would laugh at the "Seven-Hundred Club" and others who seemed more interested in profit than prophesy. In the 1980's he would recant, chuckling, the tearful confession of Jimmy Swaggart. "Caught red-handed," Daddy'd laugh. "Prostitute and a flat tire. Tee-hee-hee. Forgive'm. Send 'im some more money."

Gail and I joined in the laughter. "Hey, you know what we

say – never trust a man with high hair," Gail chimed, chuckling.

"Yeh, boy," agreed Daddy. "The higher they is, the harder they fall. Point is, never trust a Christian who's askin' for money."

From his recliner, Daddy sat in judgment as little by little the kingdom of television evangelism fell apart. He had little sympathy for Jim and Tammy Faye Bakker. Daddy wasn't alone, though. All of us cackled at the almost *Saturday-Night-Live* daily news of the Fall. This should have been a sign unto us: For those who think too highly of themselves, who sit in judgment of others, surely will get their comeuppance in life.

And I watched, with more than a casual chortle, my father as his back bowed and his knees "gave out," as he would say. More than once I noted how very much he and George Wallace looked alike. I wondered how much of the "fightin' little judge from Clio, Alabama," was really left.

In my dreams I tried to reconcile the different versions of my father. I could be thirteen again, forced to attend whatever church rally or political convention Daddy deemed necessary at the time.

Sometimes, on a Sunday night after the evening service at Millbrook Baptist Church, we would go to Hazel Liveoak's house. After Mama had played for church, and we had sung "Bringing in the Leaves" or "Stanley on the Promises," Gail's and my version of the familiar Baptist tunes, we would dance along as Mama played "Yes, Sir, That's My Baby." Hazel would shimmy in her nightgowns and hats, sometimes dancing the Charleston as her own daughters joined in. They could dance at Hazel's house, even though the Baptists didn't approve. Fact is, the Baptist held a Sweet Heart Banquet in February so the girls wouldn't go to the high-school dance and be tempted by the devil himself.

But there at Hazel's house, Hazel and all of us, except Daddy, who was still railroading back and forth to Mobile, would dance along and laugh as Mama played the piano. There was laughter when Daddy was away in Mobile. Hazel could always make Mama laugh. I always thought she was like Mama's sister, only less Baptist maybe – she didn't believe in all of the Apostle Paul's submission business, and she even had a state job. Mama's playing would get faster and faster and Hazel finally tossed off her shoes. Pretty soon, everyone was dancing. Gail and I would slide across the floor and nearly hit the floor furnace. And I knew then, as I would appreciate later on, how very much Hazel was like Mama's tree of life.

# XIX

## Welcome to Slapout, Alabama

One side of the road-side advertisement announced, "Welcome to Holtville." Another said, "Welcome to Slapout." Whether you called the community Slapout or Holtville depended on whom you were trying to impress. When they were talking to regular folk, like railroaders and singers, and had plenty of time for explaining, Joe and Lois said home was Slapout. Then they'd smile. Everybody would. But when they were at a funeral or doctor's office, they said Holtville. Sometimes not having to explain the locality came in handy. For example, if someone asked, "Where do you live?" Joe and Lois might respond, "Slapout."

Then the conversation would follow a predictable point of almost no return, and the legendary Boys' Store would be mentioned to explain just how Slapout got its unofficial name. ("We're just slap out of that" was the response to inquiries about the availability of goods, the story goes.)

It was rather like the joke Ebbie Barrington told Gail and me as kids. "Pete and Repeat were sitting on a fence. Pete fell off. So who was left?" We would eventually have to turn our heads to avoid his jack-o-lantern smile and the inevitable repetition of the Pete and Repeat joke.

Regardless, Slapout, also known as Holtville to avoid redundancy, was the community where Mama and Daddy moved to retire. For the first time, they embraced a compromise.

Daddy had his trolling motor, and when he wasn't fishing, he would sit on a side-porch swing where he could drink coffee, watch the sun rise, and call up birds. Whippoorwills, mocking birds, turkeys, owls – Daddy's communion with nature was uncanny, and it was private.

Mama too had privacy in the shared compromise. She could fish alone, as she often did, although she sometimes trolled for bass along Lake Jordan with my father, usually in late evening. At other times Mama spent days and money freely at the Santuck flea market. For once Daddy didn't say anything about her bringing home junk or spending too much, and she was excessive in both ways.

And then there were the singing birds, one of which was always perched upon Mama's shoulder even as she cooked. Mama seemed indifferent to the fluttering feathers that sometimes ended up in the cornmeal mix. The birds echoed a newfound joy for both Mama and Daddy. One bird stayed with Daddy inside and whistled whenever Mama came in as it called, "Oh, Lois! Wh- whheww! I'm a pretty boy!"

The lakeside yard held a variety of plastic flamingoes and odd pieces of discards turned into makeshift flower pots, the most notable a Christmas cactus planted in a barbeque grill. In the flower beds were brightly colored, plastic windmills that added rustic charm. Daddy called them a "cuss-sundry." And then there were Daddy's own copious mounds of broken bricks – which Gail called "Daddy's Project." The plan was to use the bricks as some sort of retaining wall by the lake, but that project never got off the ground. Instead, truckloads were simply tossed off the riverbank, while others were used to border flowerbeds. Still others Mama turned into paths that led to the water. Dogwood lined the trail, and Mama planted an assortment of exotic plants that bloomed once a day or at midnight. Neither she nor the neighbor, Asenyth, who became a lifelong best friend, ever missed a bloom.

Life was good.

In the early 1980's the Regan years brought the promise of peace to the world, even to Slapout, where Mama and Daddy had made their peace. The dissolution of the Cold War had begun. I too was ready to dissolve the cold wars. The marriage I'd run to when I left home didn't last long. Within a few years, I was ready to start again, to bring my new baby to the lake, to reclaim a portion of happiness I'd not had earlier. That was not to happen, though. My dreams of returning to school, living on the lake with Mama and Daddy, truly starting over – Daddy soon doused.

"You've made your bed; now you've got to lie in it," familiar lines from Daddy. "Your mother has raised her children," more familiar lines which could be translated, "and she won't raise yours." At other times he would say, "I didn't ask you to get married, and I aint asking you to get divorced," all voiced to Mama's background of "Oh, Joe," and "I'm sorry, Susie."

After the short marriage, I borrowed money from Daddy to get a divorce. My daughter was less than a year old. That same summer, I sold a washing machine, repaid Daddy, and moved out. My ninety days of freedom, of hoping to reclaim and share their newfound joy on Lake Jordan, came to an abrupt end. Mama wept the day I left. It was not the first time I had left without looking back, hearing her sobs in the background. Her tears were more than I could stand. Daddy sniffed nervously, but he didn't budge. He reminded me that my job now was "to take care of little Stephanie." That, he said, was my most important job, not school, not happiness, but "seeing after" my little daughter. That's what he'd always done, he told me. At that moment, I didn't see things that way, though. He warned me to stay away from alcohol and to put Stephanie first, because if I didn't, my little mama would. It was a promise and a threat, one I would later earmark as a significant epiphany in my becoming adult.

At the time, I didn't truly understand that my father had taught me more than I would ever be able to thank him for or acknowledge in so many words. In many ways, his wisdom shaped my adult life in ways I could never have imagined. Slowly, I would learn to accept his wisdom, though it would be years before acknowledging it as such.

But I learned to keep quiet, and as I did so, I learned acceptance and thanksgiving. Though I couldn't tell my own parents, I was grateful for them. I was thankful for my daughter and the chance we had to make a life together, thankful for the peace everyone found. Stephanie became the bridging compromise. There by the river, the new bridge  between generations connected us as no other.

In the three years I was a single parent, Joe and Lois were the village. When Stephanie was sick, Mama was always there to help. "No" just wasn't in her vocabulary, and Pop, too, did whatever he could to help his grandchild, the only one my parents had  in the state of Alabama. The bond formed during those years was unshakable, unforgettable.  Daddy never tired of reading Pooh books or Brer Rabbit stories to Stephanie. And he always came over to cut my grass – he insisted, even after I bought my own lawn mower.

A new era had begun, a change in both Daddy and me.  I grew up, not without struggle or difficulty.

And Joe Lee, Joe Lee mellowed.

The rewards for all of us were many. Before long, the  greatest gift of all, Dwan, and soon a second daughter, Allison– a sister for Stephanie –  all led me to openly say, "thank you, Lord." Perhaps even more importantly, I found a way to at least silently acknowledge,  "Thank you, Joe Lee." I couldn't tell him yet, though, and I wonder now if I ever did.

Morning and evening were the first of many to come, and I found joy. We all did. Dwan would fish, listen to Daddy for hours, fix odd pieces of equipment that Mama had managed to destroy.

"Couldn't be better," Dwan said. In Mama and Daddy, he found the parents he had lost early in life, and they too found a son to love.

Life was good.

By the still waters of the lake, Stephanie and Allison experienced summers with their grandparents, Joe and Lois– Ma Lee and Pop– for whom the clock signaled nothing more than lunch or supper. By the still waters of the summertime lake, the girls searched for rocks, caught their first fish, learned to swim, though their grandmother could not.

And when nap time or evening came, Stephanie and Allison heard the Pop stories told by the fire or on the porch, much as I had listened to them only a few years before. My girls spent much of their childhood listening to my father spin yarns and tell railroad stories. And they spent a great deal of time with my mother, gleaning the secrets of the Coosa along its rocky bank. For once, Mama could experience the joy of unconditional, unfettered adoration in her new role as an adventurous grandmother.

Pop slowly changed somewhat. When I asked him to refrain from using the "n" word around my children and me, he sometimes respected my request, though more often he would just apologize after he had slipped. When I explained to Stephanie and Allison that their grandfather was from another generation, they accepted that, as only children can do.

For once, my mother had her peace on Earth. I told Mama she'd finally found the River Jordan. My daughters tagged along with her, exploring rocks on the shoreline, searching for bargains at flea markets, or whatever adventure the day brought. In my mother, my own children found fearlessness.

I remember my mother phoning me at work, laughing as she recounted the summertime's afternoon activity. She and the girls had been digging for fishing worms in a leaf bed by a bay tree when Stephanie suddenly squealed, "Ma Lee, snake! Snake, Ma Lee."

"No, they're just big earth worms," Mama reassured her

granddaughters as she reached down with her scoop to retrieve the squiggling brown mass of what she assumed were worms.

" Don't touch the snake, Ma Lee."

Stephanie kept whining, and by then Allison had run back to the house.

Mama dropped her scoop, grabbed Stephanie, and ran into the house, laughing. She was still laughing when she called me. I can almost hear her now.

"They were pygmy rattlers," Mama emphasized, "not worms!"

"I don't think that's funny, Mama," I said. "What other perilous activities do you have planned for my daughters today?"

"Nothing but fishing!" she exclaimed. "We'll just use plastic worms."

"Don't forget the life jackets," I warned, but Mama had already hung up the telephone receiver. She claimed Stephanie's first words had been "boat ride" and thought nothing of letting either granddaughter perch on the tall fishing seat at the front of the bass boat as they skipped across Lake Jordan, full throttle, the bow high.

"They can see better up there," Mama defended when I protested. Not knowing how to swim never dampened Mama's affinity for deep water and fishing boats. Nor did it make her cling to a life-preserver.

"Too hot," she'd say. "They get in the way when I cast. Don't you have any faith, Susie?"

"Yes, I have faith," I said, "but you really test it. Please be careful."

What she loved most of all about Lake Jordan was her private time on the lake. Each evening after dinner, when she had "fed Joe," as she said, Mama donned her frayed fishing hat, a Thermos of iced tea, Pall Malls, and laughed. "Gone fishing," she'd chuckle as she headed to the pier, waving behind her back.

Her responses to concerns about her safety were predictable. "This is my time of the day – don't you have any faith?"

Michael insisted on the most developed technology of the day and placed a "bag phone" on the yellow bass boat. But Mama never plugged it in.

Nine p.m. My phone would ring. "Your li'l mama aint back yet. Mighty worried about her," Daddy would say.

"Well, Daddy, I reckon she's all right. She's got a phone. What do you want me to do – look for her?"

"She caint swim a lick."

"There's nothing I can do, Daddy. She's your wife," I would add.

"Confound the luck." Daddy would give up. Finally, Mama would call me after she came in from a night of fishing. She had just lost track of time. She apologized for Daddy's calls. She apologized for worrying anyone.

But she had her secret joys.

# XX

## Epiphany

She waited. I don't know how. My mother's heart failure on the fiftieth anniversary of Pearl Harbor occurred at the very same time Daddy was being wheeled away to emergency heart surgery. Caught in a crisis of her own, Mama was unaware that Daddy too faced peril. What had been explained as a relatively simple procedure of using a stint to unblock Daddy's heart turned into open-heart surgery. I was alone with Daddy, thinking Mama had probably overslept.

My father's heart was opened that day as he humbled himself to the great equalizer of life – suffering, pain, near-death experiences, the realization that life is tenuous.

It was a defining moment. I saw something in Daddy's eyes that I had never before seen. We had only a few seconds together before he was wheeled away to emergency surgery. Before then I had never known my father to show fear. As he trembled, I held his hand and tried to assure him that he would be okay. I did not know, but I could not let him see my doubt. As I took his glasses and kissed him on his sweating brow, I saw the silent stream of tears follow the crease of his neck, and I too was afraid.

Something about our lives had changed forever.

Downstairs, alone in the emergency room, my mother held out as she always could, willing herself into surviving just long enough to put others first. She had collapsed in the parking lot. Her heart had failed again, and even when Michael, Wayne, and Gail arrived, we didn't have the courage to tell her about Daddy's heart surgery, which thankfully had gone well. "Oh, Daddy's doing just fine, just fine," all of us assured her. Daddy's condition was such that it really wasn't until a week later that he had the presence of mind to ask about Mama.

A week later, though, when we felt that Mama and Daddy were strong enough to know what had happened to the other, we wheeled Mama into Daddy's hospital room. And each faced an individual version of truth and somehow knew that from this moment on their lives would be forever altered. They faced their own mortality.

Mama's greatest fear was that one of us would have to take care of Daddy, and her sheer determination seemed to heal her. She willed herself into recovery.

And so Mama held out somehow, as she always had, and waited while both she and Daddy slowly recovered. She waited because she knew she had to.

Three months later, she arrived by ambulance at University Hospital in Birmingham, tenuously hanging to life by wires and monitors that could have done little to save her. Miraculously, she held on to life. She would need two heart valves.

We waited, and waited, and waited. For hours we waited. But some things could not wait. While Mama's life was suspended in open-heart surgery, Daddy had more pressing issues. He had a hang nail. Did I have a nail file? Could I get one? Could I find hearing-aid batteries? I will never forget the compassionate volunteer who found hearing-aid batteries amid the maze of the huge hospital. That appeased Daddy for a while, at least until it was time for a little snack. Some fresh coffee. Then, to be sure, lunch had to be considered. Could we help him find the bathroom? Would we wait? Gail and I took turns taking care of Daddy while the other watched and waited, and waited, and waited, talked to incoming relatives, and took calls to address unanswerable questions about Mama's condition.

We faced Mama's life and death by the minute while Daddy

watched the clock to see when it was time to eat again

If given the choice to see Mama for the last time at noon, I do believe Daddy would have said some things just can't be settled on an empty stomach. Gail and I told Daddy he was like Pooh Bear.

Finally, all of us settled down in the waiting room, another great equalizer. From time to time, I would go outside, clutch a strange chain-linked fence between two buildings, and utter the Lord's Prayer. I felt alone in my fear. Still I cried, prayed, clutched the fence and waited on the Lord.

Daddy, on the other hand, talked. And talked. And talked. Once, when we took him on a family vacation, my husband and I took turns listening to Daddy as the girls slept and read *Tales of a Fourth-Grade Nothing* over and over and over. For ten hours, Daddy talked all the way to Orlando, Florida. Dwan likes to tell the story now.

So it was that day in the waiting room. My father talked.

In any gathering of people, my father was the kind of person who would introduce himself, tell too much personal history – how he retired from the L&N, where he grew up, married in 1941, way too much about his "little daughters," grandchildren, and the like. By the same token, within ten minutes, he'd learned where the other person grew up, what he or she did to make a living, how many children and grandchildren there were, political party affiliation, and so on. We could time how quickly he could establish the exact kinship of a seeming stranger. I think the record was three minutes.

On that great day of equalization, the good Lord placed right beside my father a black man as old as Daddy. Like my father, he carried a cane proudly. Like my father, he wore a suit and tie in public. Like my father, his wife had just had open heart surgery. Both men sat calmly, smiling as they reassured each other. The two found very much in common, and my father did not notice the race of his new friend, whose name must have been Moses.

Moses's wife had surgery weeks ago, but she was still in intensive care. "Been on a resprator twelve days," he said.

"Show nuff?" my father asked sincerely. "Just have to hope and pray," he added.

"Yup, hope and pray," said Moses.

Mama's surgery lasted nearly all day, and she had heart surgery a second time the next day, this time in a truly emergency situation. My sister arrived with Daddy, expecting to see Mama recovering from the previous day's surgery. But they were too late to see her because she had been wheeled away again. I was relieved that no one had seen her, because she had seemed so near death that I didn't want to frighten Daddy and Gail.

And so this time I alone did the worrying and watching. Daddy had biscuits while Mama had surgery again, this time to stop the bleeding of her heart.

Always in the same chair sat Moses whenever Daddy returned from his most recent feeding. And so began the ritual of their friendship, Daddy and Moses, finding common ground in the peril of their suffering wives and lives. The two men's canes were identical, as were their hats and hopes.

"Just hope and pray," said Moses.

"'Bout all you can do, hope and pray for the best," said Daddy.

Mama slowly recovered, and she refused to let anyone help her. She pulled the covers over her head as the doctors and nurses tried to talk to her.

"What? What?" she would call as though from some other lifetime. Surely she was not trapped in this pain; she would escape.

But like an injured wild animal, she would not let anyone near her – including me.

"Mrs. Lee?" the nurses shouted. I watched from the doorway, my arms folded. The nurses bent down close to my mother's face as they tried to elicit a response from her.

"She can hear," I would tell them. "She just doesn't want to now." I always knew my mother too well, and I was too tired to pretend.

Meanwhile, each day Daddy met Moses in the lobby. Through the many hours of coffee and waiting, they talked, and talked, and talked. I didn't have to say anything at all, and was relieved.

"Looks like he's found 'im another railroad buddy," Gail remarked.

"A union man– the Brotherhood." We laughed together.

The third miracle happened on the eighth day. It was homecoming day for Mama. Daddy and I arrived to take Mama home when we met Moses on the elevator.

"Well, how's ya wife today, Mistuh Lee?" asked Moses, smiling as he leaned slightly on his cane.

"Doin' fine, doin' fine," said Daddy. "Goin' home today! How's your wife?"

"She's off the resprator. Breathin' on her own. Aint it a blessing?" Moses exclaimed.

"Well, I do declare!" agreed Daddy.

"It's all a blessin', a blessin' of the Lord," said Moses.

"Aint it?" echoed Daddy.

As Moses got off the elevator, Daddy turned to me and said, "You know, I think race relations is better than they've ever been in this country."

" It's all a blessin'," I said, smiling.

# XXI

## Homecoming

After my parents' hearts were opened for repair, in some sense I felt that I too needed time to allow my spirit and heart to change. Not only did I want to spend more time with them, but I wanted to take the roads back to their roots, to be part of the journey, to be able to write about it as an imbedded scribe.

And so, more than once, we went back to Butler County, my parents, my children, and I. As my parents took turns telling their stories, I too made note of the ones I had heard before, of the journeys I had taken. These became a part of the written chronicles I soon began to share; I was shaping new words to share familiar songs. And for a few suspended hours, it seemed like all of Alabama was listening. The journey was a step back in time and place.

As a child, I had always imagined that the road had been scribbled into the green hillside in the road that led for miles, where you turned from Georgiana to go to Garland, Alabama.

The route to Granny's was along a winding, narrow path of paved country road that had been cut through red clay, the kind of soil that "wouldn't grow nothin'," my father always had said. County Road 8 had more curves and hills and dangerous blind spots than one could ever design. We always took that green road slowly, never more than 25 miles an hour.

Before my birth, my father, in his new green, uninsured, four-door 1953 Chevrolet, had met a gang of drunks head-on around one blind curve, Dilly Hill. The car had been thrown into a kudzu-covered ravine, and my infant sister flung from my mother's arms, miraculously unharmed.

It was a lesson my father always shared each time we took that turn toward Garland. We always marveled at the miracle of how the young family's life had been spared as Daddy, chuckling, cautioned us to insure one's car in more than the Lord and other drivers. There were so many lessons shared back then, and even now as we headed to the Garland Church for Homecoming a generation later. My eight-year-old daughter Allison stood to see the countryside her grandparents and great-grandparents had called home. Stephanie, by now thirteen, bore a striking resemblance to me when I was her age. As she sat in the back seat, writing in her journal, I wondered what stories she would tell. I knew she was listening.

We took the interstate that day, though later I would take that old road back toward Georgiana alone. I wanted to see that scribbled path, to take it back through what had been a dominant childhood memory. I wanted to feel again the excitement of rounding a steep curve without knowing what might be beyond, yet knowing I would be happy to see it. I wanted to see the kudzu-green ravine and red clay bank where death nearly had been met in the topside-down 1953 Chevrolet.

From Interstate 65, one had a choice to exit left to Garland or right to the community of Grace, where some said Hiram Williams had lived and, some said, fled. We went the other way, to Garland Church.

Taking that road to Granny's house as a child, I always would stand up in the backseat of our white 1960 Bel Aire at the first sight of a railroad crossing. That marked we were almost there, that railroad crossing, the same crossing Daddy had passed every other day for nearly forty years as a brakeman on the L&N Railroad.

When she heard the train, my aunt would wave from the front door of the matchbox-sized post office where she had worked nearly a lifetime. She raced to see the train. My father would wave triumphantly as he held close to the caboose. Sometimes, he boasted, he would walk atop the rail cars and could light a cigarette even at 60 miles an hour.

My grandmother too would watch from the front porch of her house next to the post office. Mr. Joe must have been something of a hero riding that train through Garland, waving at farmers he'd known all his life as they hoed and tilled the soil in the August heat that lasted well into fall. Each trip across the home rails was a victory ride that always reminded him of the poverty and hopelessness he had wanted to overcome by leaving Butler County.

Days after the Japanese bombed Pearl Harbor, he had taken my mother from the quiet religious folds of south Alabama to the big city of Montgomery where a woman could work, if her husband would let her, at H.L. Green's or Montgomery Fair, to the better life all envisioned.

Like that day so many years ago, today in Butler County was the Lord's Day. No one tilled the soil, and the only sound was that our car made as it thudded twice over the rails at the Garland, Alabama, crossing. The silence of age seemed settled in the abandoned grass and ash-colored ric-rac beside the tracks. Few trains came through now, my father said.

He was nearly eighty years old now. I wondered what he thought as we passed the crossing, as he relived the vision in silence.

"Where's your train, Pop?" asked both daughters at once.

"It'll be along t'rectly," he said.

My daughters too were taking that journey in silence, one they had heard so much about. I imagined I was as young again as they were. Living father north in Alabama, I never saw my aunt come outside to wave at my father every other day at 2:05 p.m. as Number 2759 faithfully sounded, yet I've imagined the scene so many times, surely I was there.

Next door I would have seen my grandmother rocking on the front porch of the house, dipping snuff, spitting off the side into tall south Alabama camellias.

"Did you call your grandmother 'Zillie Mae'? " my oldest daughter asked.

"No, but that was her name. You don't hear of too many grandmothers named Zillie Mae anymore," I responded.

As we drove toward the church where Homecoming was to be observed today, a generation after my grandmother's death, I could hear her boast of being one-quarter Creek. She would tell of how she had broken the only doll she'd ever had in childhood, a porcelain doll that must stay on the mantel, her mother had said.

I would remember riding with my grandmother throughout Butler County in some large green car with clear-plastic-covered seats. How adventuresome she had been. I remember thinking that I didn't really notice when she became old, because we had simply known her no other way, and despite her energies, she simply died one day before a youth could understand what illness and age and time really meant, before I understood the value of her story about the China doll. A Chinaberry tree in front of her old place outlived her, only to remind me of the strong-willed girl my grandmother had been, a girl who'd silently stolen the China doll off the mantel and shattered it into hundreds of unrecognizable pieces. Looking back now, I could really see the proud Creek in my grandmother, especially as she rocked in her later years, focusing straightaway at something I could not see. She rocked, she sang, she played only the white keys on the piano, and talked about faith and being glory-bound. Somewhere, not too far from here, she was buried silently in the same small crossroads of her birth, the same place as my mother's birth, Owassa. The Indian name, the unexplained history – the silence seemed fitting for the grandmother I had so often observed rocking, rocking, rocking.

Taking that road to Garland today, I missed her more now than ever before, wanted to tell her how much one grows older and older and yearns to know the hearts of those who could make everything make sense. Those thoughts are that much sought-after title to a fond tune one keeps humming, trying to remember the words.

My grandmother, who'd learned to drive upon her sixtieth birthday, had always been stubborn but self-reliant. My grandfather had been a "revenue officer" in the army of the Lord, stomping out the power of sin by uncovering whiskey stills hidden in the Butler County bottomlands during Prohibition.

His was a job that had kept him out late. Sometimes, real or imagined threats would prompt my grandmother, Zillie Mae, to instruct her children to hide as she would take her pearl-handled .32 pistol and shoot wildly out the windows. Dogs barked and ran under the porch, and her children sought shelter underneath the kitchen table. Afterward, I imagine Granny quoted scripture, though the only scripture I remember her ever quoting was that about how the Lord had told Timothy to take a little wine for his stomach's sake.

There were new pictures today of old memories, of how I had often heard her sing at the nursing home in her last years. She would sing a few measures, hum a few of "Leaning on the Everlasting Arms" and "What a Friend We Have in Jesus." She would clamor them out on the off tune piano.

"One day," she encouraged me, "you'll learn how to play all the black notes."

Today, my father talked of how he had met my mother on so many occasions. Mostly he talked of her father, my grandfather Countryman who had taught shaped notes, even made $8 at his singing school, pretty good in those days, Daddy always remembered.

Hank Williams had studied with Brother Countryman, the conversation always went, and had been unable to pay his own way. In the recollection of our portrait pasts, there is that moment of wonder, of having brushed some color of greatness as a silent and uncredited artist.

My aunt had played the piano as my grandfather taught four-part harmony to teens like Hank and my father, as my mother, only eight years old or so then, listened outside with the silent sort of envy only children know.

Now we would follow the road through Garland to the church where, when the end of Prohibition had dried up my grandfather's income as a revenue officer, he had answered the call to preach. More than fifty years after his death, we were there for Homecoming. Only a handful, thirty or so, gathered.

It was here at the Garland Church that my grandfather must have won a few souls to Christ as my grandmother hammered out "Just as I Am" on the only piano the church ever had, one she donated. It was here my eighty-year-old aunt still played every Sunday with the same commitment she'd held for more than fifty years in the Baptist Women's Union. We sat beside the stained glass window that bore a memorial to an uncle who'd died in a car accident the weekend he celebrated his return from the Korean War. The blue-pink circle showed Jesus with children at His knee.

But if the Lord were to come today, his call would not be heard by my youngest daughter, who'd laid her head in my lap. I ran my fingers through her blond curls as she fell asleep with the soundness and ease so characteristic of small children during a church service.

"We'd like to extend a special welcome to all of you who've come home," said Brother Sellers.

His face was aged and familiar. This had been his church too after my grandfather died, at least every fifth Sunday when he could also look forward to dinner with my grandmother and aunt. I wondered if he remembered me as the five-year-old who had clanked repeated tunes in the key of C as the family gathered for Sunday dinner with the preacher.

Now he spoke of the families who'd gone to a heavenly palace filled with streets of gold, and he called them by name - Zillie Mae, Brother Countryman, and their young son who fought communism so valiantly. Sellers welcomed back all of God's people, including Brother Joe and his family. He said we were all called to a great homecoming. I wanted to listen as he talked about so many rooms in our Father's mansion in a special place already prepared, but in the one-room church, I envisioned my grandmother playing that piano. I wanted to imagine what my grandfather must have looked like as he preached the gospel. I never met him, since he met the Maker long before I was born.

Homecoming Sunday in Garland, Alabama: I played the heavy upright piano as my aunt, father, and mother sang in a country harmony where all breathed together, and leaned toward Daddy as he voiced the melody. They must have remembered being early teens again, must have remembered others who had oftentimes sung with them, friends long since resting in peace for that great day of resurrection.

I too wanted to sing about a heavenly mansion just over the hilltop that Homecoming Day in Garland, but it was time to observe, to embrace the lessons missed by not going back sooner. Such peace. I wondered how it must have been for my parents to leave. How hard it must have been for my father to come back and leave again, to have its memories wave at you from the porch every other day; to know that no matter how often you returned, since you'd left, you'd always be an outsider.

There was dinner on the grounds following the service. Soon, above the buzz of an old, old family reunited, came the sound of a train as it approached the Garland crossing. A whistle blew again, its distant rumbling beckoning. The sound of a train approaching in the countryside is like no other. No highway traffic clamors to compete with its solo; no cargo jets thunder overhead. Instead, the train's echoing melody is one of a distant tune; then one hears the sound of tracks buckling as steel-rail cars cross. If you listen closely, my father always said, sounds tell just how fast a train is coming, or where it must slow down.

"Listen," my father said now.

It was only a train, and there were pies down the long wooden tables that reached from tree to tree, tables laden with food only once a year at the Garland Church.

"Move along. Move along if you can, Ol' Josephus," my mother said.

But there would be plenty of time for sweet potato pie and greens. I watched as my father walked toward the crossing to see the train, as though eye to eye.

"It's Number 2759," he said as he looked at his railroad watch.

The whistle blew again to warn any passing automobiles that the train was about to cross the Garland, Alabama, road, though there would be so few to pass on this Lord's Day. If only he could raise his right arms now, he could wave as the train passed, this time with no caboose. Biggest mistake the railroad ever made, he said, doing away with the caboose.

Number 2759 called again as it had for years.

Like that eight-year-old listening outside as her father taught harmony, I watched as my father walked alone toward the call that was at once destiny and memory. He smiled.

He turned to see me, but I stood back. This was his moment, his call, as it had been so long ago.

"Right on time," he said with quiet satisfaction.

And I knew, I knew that day as though for the first time, Daddy had heard something others had not really heard. He embraced it as he had so many years ago in some way others just didn't understand. But I did. He heard his call. I heard it too.

And Joe Lee never missed a call.

# XXII

## Silence

In the fall of 1989, we sat transfixed as cable news broadcast the new fall of Berlin. Mobs from the east converged with those from the west to raze the very symbol of the Cold War itself, the Berlin Wall. None of us could actually believe what we were seeing. CNN had changed the way we would view world events. We could no longer perceive them academically, or apathetically. Instead, we were live witnesses made participants, and the real-time coverage imposed a sense of responsibility and duty. Once again, something about our lives had changed forever.

As I watched, I was reminded of the counterbalance of historical events and my family's lives, how pivotal points seemed to coincide with those in my family, how, looking back at least, I had always turned to those events as historical mile markers.

In the blur of memory, all of it seemed to happen at once, the crumbling of communism and socialism, but it was actually months later that in the Soviet Union a coup d'etat deposed Mikhail Gorbachev. We watched CNN in disbelief as Boris Yeltsin waved from atop a tanker and reveled his way to victory. Angry crowds stormed Red Square, toppling icons in a scene that would foreshadow the demise of Saddam Hussein in the second war with Iraq a decade later.

What Mama said so many years ago was still true: we were watching history. The United States had fought three wars to achieve this final victory, the ultimate defeat of communism, and for the first time in my lifetime, genuine peace seemed imminent. But I silently wondered if I were the only skeptic. I honestly believed that the Communists, or some other dictatorial form of power, would crush the crowds in Red Square just as they had at China's Tiananmen Square.

No one wants to admit so now, but there were many skeptics, especially in the days during which Gorbachev was held from power. Everyone was uncertain that Yeltsin would really bring freedom. How could the Cold War, which had been such a presence throughout so many decades, suddenly disappear? The unspoken fear was that West Germany and the Soviet Union would be overtaken, perhaps by China, yet everyone was so excited about the end of the Cold War that we kept our doubts private.

We would soon learn that the Cold War had been a safer world where we at least knew our enemies.

As the Cold War dissolved, the unspeakable tension in my own family grew. No one could quite identify the source of the tension, but it was evident nevertheless.

Inexplicably, everyone in my family coordinated his or her visits with our parents when no other siblings might be present. Michael's and Wayne's visits were planned specifically to avoid confrontation with each other. Gail and I could not get along, and she invariably found a way to blame Mama and Daddy for all her adult problems. She blamed her imperfect childhood on Mama, Daddy, Michael, and me. All of us were at fault for her current unhappiness. Often there were explosions during her brief visits.

"Well, I'm glad you're perfect, Susie – you always were chosen," she might scream through her tears before leaving, again, in the midst of another holiday dinner. When our own children were stunned by her behavior, my mother pleaded with Gail to look at what she was doing.

What we failed to see was that Gail had the courage we lacked, that her own anger was ours, that she was our voice and conscience. It was just easier to pretend that she – not any of us – had the problem.

From Gail came the rage for which Mama felt so responsible. Always the diplomat, the peacemaker, I tried to convince Mama and Gail to put the past behind them. But Mama bore the guilt of generations, for not getting Gail and me out of what was undoubtedly an unhappy childhood home where conflicts abounded, even conflicts I never acknowledged or faced. And while Gail tried to confront the family  demons, I was still hiding behind a wall of silence, trying to make everything okay by simply pretending there were no problems or that by bringing them up now, we stood nothing to gain.  Gail told me I had done this for so long that I no longer even knew the truth. Though she quite likely was right, what could I do now? I wondered. What was to be gained?

While elsewhere in the world the Cold War was ending, in some ways it had only begun at home.

Still I tried to comfort Mama. She was aging. "Gail's grown now," I said. "We all are – and there's nothing we can do to change the past, Mama. You did the best you could. So did Daddy. Gail and I, Michael and Wayne – we all have children of our own. We're all adults."

What Gail verbalized, Wayne never did. Instead, he kept a safe distance to avoid the cold war at home. The dysfunction perhaps so well hidden in adolescence now left irreversible scars  in adulthood for all of us. And so, for  many, many years, Wayne simply would not come home. It was the way he had learned to survive. Gail and I were envious.

"They stole my childhood, yours too – you just won't admit it," charged Gail. By now, I didn't even know what she meant. At least I could pretend. But I didn't know the truth, not really, and I wasn't sure there was an exact point to which I could claim things had gone terribly wrong in our family. Mama and  Daddy were facing their own mortality, but there was nothing I  could do about any of it. I wanted to try, though. Nothing ever kept me from trying.

In our silence or safe distance, all of us  learned to survive the cold war in Alabama. The easiest way was to simply avoid facing the truth, whatever or whoever that might be. We could not topple the wall that divided us, and so each of us simply practiced what we knew best: avoidance.

The simple blunder of it all came down to one of numbers, of reconciling the fact that Mama had chosen to stay fifty years with a man she inwardly and outwardly conceded had been the wrong choice all along. Somewhere in all of this her children were supposed to make her happy and her grandchildren bring joy to a joyless union.

Christmas Eve, 1991, just weeks after their joint hospitalizations: it was my parents' fiftieth wedding anniversary. Mama had made me promise that we wouldn't hold any kind of party or reception.

"There's nothing to celebrate, Susie— and I mean that. Don't do anything for us," she insisted. There was anger in her voice. She wasn't feigning reluctance in order to enjoy a surprise party later.

"But doesn't just staying with someone for fifty years count for something?" I asked. "Surely you've had some good times together, Mama."

"I did it for you girls, and it's been a living hell on Earth," Mama said adamantly.

There are some matters in life for which a mother's children can't just say "I'm sorry," expect forgiveness, or find redemption. The deeply rooted guilt for my mother's unhappiness was one I had been trying to rectify since adolescence, but it would be one I would never reconcile. Instead, my mother handed me her burden and I held it deep within, like a decaying wisdom tooth whose twisted roots bore their way through my jaw and jarred my whole being.

Blessed are the peacemakers.

Instead of having a fifty-year anniversary reception or party or even a reunion with all the family, Mama and Daddy spent Christmas Eve alone, silenced. Mama didn't feel like entertaining and wanted no company. There was to be no peace on Earth that year.

I visited them alone because others, quite rightfully, didn't want to commiserate. When I arrived that dismal evening, I found Daddy sipping soup in solitude as he watched television from his recliner. He tried to warm himself by the wood-burning stove that covered what had once been an ornate fireplace. On the stove, a kettle of water steamed.

"Your little mama is mighty unhappy," Daddy said. "Reckon she don't feel good."

"I guess so," I said. There were no words.

Later, by phone, Gail offered her own advice. "Just take care of Susie. You can't make them happy."

Gail was right – I couldn't make anyone happy, but I wasn't listening yet. Something inside compelled me – maybe I was still hoping for the *Leave It To Beaver* family from my childhood television memories.

I wanted to see good where perhaps there was none; happiness where perhaps there was only a void. I wanted to fix Mama, to appease Gail, to make things right in the family by being the centerpiece, the piano player, the entertainer, the peacemaker.

Something gnawed inside – the inner anguish, the sense of responsibility for Gail's and Mama's pain; for Daddy's discontent. It was that compulsion to want to fix everyone, to bring Gail home in time for Christmas – it never went away.

It was the same feeling I had as a child when I ran off and left Gail in the field, stepping on black runners, itching from the tall Johnson grass, or like the time I rode to the top of the County Road 7 hill. There I could look south and see the Alabama River and the state capitol, but behind me was only that red-dirt road where trees formed a canopy of shade overhead. Looking down and back that seemingly peaceful portrait of childhood, I couldn't see or bring back my family, a family Gail said we never really had. She was quite likely right.

I could not bring peace because some walls can't be torn down and are protective retainers anyway.

"There's good and bad in everybody," Daddy said without looking up. It was quite likely the closest he would ever come to admitting he had been a difficult husband and father.

As I listened to the silence between what he didn't say or couldn't say, I wondered how I could learn to be silent, to quietly accept what I could not change, to acknowledge that perhaps everyone else had been right all along about this secret cold war.

If only I had conceded that some things in life can never change.

# XXIII

## Responsibility

My father had been splitting wood and stacking it into enviable columns the day he had the first stroke. He was eighty years old. The day I got the call at work was like any other, but for the fact that our lives would change forever from that moment on. The time I waited for Michael to arrive seemed an eternity.

As Michael and I stayed with him in the hospital for three weeks, Daddy would alternate complaints about how he'd never walk again and how his chainsaw would rust if someone didn't remember to put it up.

I wondered if my father was as embarrassed as I was for him during the time he could not even go to the bathroom without help. Three weeks in the hospital I stayed with Daddy, as Dwan, Michael, and I all alternated shifts of duty.

Mama could not bear the smell of hospital, nor did she have the patience or strength to deal with my father. That job, as usual, was left to others – like Michael, Dwan, and me. When it seemed everyone else had gone, I stayed with Daddy.

Next came the six-week rehabilitation period, during which Daddy had to learn to walk again. It seemed we learned to walk again, Daddy and I, together. Gail would bring toys and cards and jokes during her short visits. "All right, Li'l Chap," Daddy would always laugh. Gail and Daddy shared the same sense of humor.

Then she'd turn to me and say, "Why don't you go home and take care of Susie? What are you, some sort of martyr?" She would laugh. So would Daddy.

But at the time, the rest of us found little to laugh about and in the coming months, when one hospital stay would lead to another, when one failed surgery led to more complications – pneumonia, heart failure, bleeding ulcers – I wondered silently,

174

as Mama verbalized, how much more Daddy could survive or the rest of us could take.

And so I tried to say nothing. Instead, I assured Daddy he would be okay, that he would walk again. I had to make him believe.

Then the unthinkable would happen as Daddy struggled through another life-threatening illness. We watched helplessly. Often, Daddy would awaken in the hospital to find Michael by his side, passing along instructions to ensure the ultimate quality recovery. And again, the unthinkable.

"Go on, Boy. Go on back home where your wife and children need you," Daddy said.

When Mama and I confronted Daddy about his thoughtless remarks to Michael, he shrugged his shoulders and sniffed. "Too much advice."

At home, Mama gave Daddy shots of Heparin while I tried to reclaim the life that had been securely Dwan's and mine pretty much away from my parents, happy in the healthy, daily ritual of raising two daughters and having a family. I longed for just a week without crisis, of not having to intervene on Mama's or Daddy's behalf.

Reclamation would be my long, hard, solitary work. Gail gave me a framed picture of Daddy beside his neat wood stacks, holding his chain saw with pride.

"Just don't do it, Susie. You know you don't have to," she remarked.

"I know," I said. By then I'd grown accustomed to the roles we'd taken in our adult lives.

For years we played the game. I would hire home health aides to care for Daddy. He couldn't raise his arms, and after his stroke, he had trouble lifting his right leg. He needed constant assistance that weighed heavily upon Mama. He would soil his clothing and sheets several times a day. Eventually, he needed a hospital bed. It became the center of what was once the dining room. All attention was focused on Daddy's needs, and so I tried to help Mama by finding people who would work. My job was to hire people.

Hers was to fire them.

The hire and fire routine went on for over five years. Mama found fault with everyone.

"Nancy Mae just sits on that couch like a lump. She smokes too much. She's too fat. I have to ask her to do everything. She's late every day." The typical complaints ran the gamut. One person might be accused of stealing or asking for money between pay checks. Another had been drinking or was unclean. "You could smell her all over the house," complained Mama, who never found fault in her untrained Yorkies. The dogs slept with her, ate from her hand at the table, and went outside only to follow Mama around as she watered flowers. She laughed when Tacky Cocoa or Iddy Biddy came inside to "do their job."

"Little stinker!" she scolded.

So, I hired people after searching for days to find someone – anyone – who could tolerate two old people with dogs and birds and cigarettes left burning in ashtrays all over the house.

"She's gone burn down the whole dagblasted house," Daddy warned.

I hired, and Mama fired. "I had to let her go. Don't you understand, Susie?" she queried.

The lake home had begun to disintegrate from need of repair. Daddy complained that he couldn't do a thing, that he was handicapped. Mama called upon Dwan, as I did, and he tried to fix whatever might be wrong. The problem was that my parents didn't want to spend any money.

"All right, half a roof," said Dwan. "I guess that's good enough.

When a faucet would go out or the back toilet might spring a leak, Dwan was expected to respond twenty four hours a day.

"Do it for me," I pleaded. "Do it for Lois. Do it for Daddy."

He insisted they call a paid repairman, but Mama and Daddy didn't want to spend the money. "You've created some kind of dependency, Susie," Dwan complained. "They can hire it done."

"It doesn't matter what you call it. They're old and they can't help it, and neither can I."

"I just can't do it all," Dwan conceded. But my parents relied upon him, upon me, to come at their call, to fix whatever was broken, to listen, to be there when no one else would. In his increasing dementia, Daddy would mistakenly call Dwan by my brothers' names, a mistake repeated even when he talked to my brothers themselves.

We moved my parents to town, just down the street from us. The loss of the lake home was personal for everyone. Gone was Lake Jordan, summer retreat, things as they were. What all of us had failed to really recognize was that little by little, our parents weren't the same as before. Sometimes I indulged in self-pity, allowed myself to feel like an only child, there alone to usher in the age of my parents' decline, always the scribe, the reporter, passing the news to an apathetic audience.

Little by little, Mama gave up what she knew best about freedom, the lake, fishing at odd hours, staying up late to watch old movies, taking off in the car to shop at flea markets and go home when she felt like it. She phoned her friends back in Slapout. "Susie did it" was the undercurrent message, and I found it hard to stay silent.

But gradually Mama claimed the new home as her own, planting crepe myrtles and hauling in fish mulch to convert the barren yard into a labyrinth of green. Banana trees soon grew taller than the house itself, and Mama's cockatoos sang from the back porch. Her Confederate roses bloomed in tri-colors, quickly capturing the interest of new neighbors. She bought a riding lawn mower, to my disapproval, and stayed outside. From time to time, she'd go inside to see what Joe needed, but not for long.

"She wont even sit down to eat. She slops food down and I have to eat it alone," Daddy complained. "She aint got time to eat. Treats me like a dog. Dogs fare better." His complaints were pitiful, and endless.

Even with hired help, Daddy insisted that Mama stay by his side. Everyone felt trapped. Caretakers tried to appease him. "I'm right here," one might say, but Daddy would call again and again.

"Lois, where's Lois?"he would keep calling. Then he would call me by phone to come down to look for her or to hear his complaints.

"I'm sorry, Daddy. I can't do anything about your wife," I joked. Daddy never saw any humor in my remarks.

# XXIV

## Let'er Go

The decision to put Daddy in a nursing home when he was eighty-four was not one my mother made, nor one she could make. Now I see that as the clues pieced together, she never fully intended any of it – she knew only what she could not do. She could not lift Daddy. She couldn't abide by his constant demands that she stay within his sight. His groaning would keep her awake all night. And there were the soiled clothes, of course. Mama spared no details in sharing how she'd managed to bathe him in the middle of the night. She was only seventy-six, and her neighbors boasted of her pioneer spirit. To me, she seemed to delight in doing yard work in the 90-degree heat so others would notice, offer to help her – she denied their assistance, of course. Sometimes neighbors called me to see if I knew what my mother was actually doing.

When I said nothing about the fact that she was on the roof or mowing the yard, they must have thought Mrs. Lee had an uncaring daughter. I never bothered explaining. Instead, I dismissed her actions. "Yeah, she's like that," I said.

By that time, I'd lost count of the number of aides Mama had fired. I had tired of hiring them and assuring them their employment rested with me.

"Don't come back. We don't need you," Mama insisted. She would pay them extra not to come. "Don't you understand, Susie?" she asked me.

"I really understand more than you give me credit for, Mama," I could honestly say. I was forty-one years old.

After Daddy's second or third stroke, I leveled with my brothers, who were understandably defensive. After all, no one wants to put his own father in a nursing home, and it wasn't something I felt I could do either.

Still, for Mama's sake, I pleaded. "Don't you understand? We have two parents." I explained about the hire-and-fire routine, and I reminded them that Joe and Lois just weren't normal people. That, they seemed to understand.

Mama kept asking, "What am I going to do, Susie?" But she refused to take part in any of the decision-making process. By then, she really meant, "Susie, what are y'all going to do?"

Wayne consoled me in the grim task that lay ahead. "I'll support you in whatever you decide. You're the one who's there every day," he said. But I couldn't do it alone. As he had so many times before, Michael drove all night long to help. In retrospect, I can appreciate him more than anyone else. He knew that Daddy would not only blame him for whatever actions were taken, but he also knew that Daddy could have stayed home if only he and Mama would cooperate. And yet, despite this knowledge, Michael came home to help. Again the silent, unsung hero, he offered to be the fall guy, to take full responsibility for the choice I thought best, but one he privately disputed. Together we carried out the most difficult mission of our lives.

Mama stayed home. I couldn't blame her.

For the first few days while Michael was still in town, Daddy enjoyed all the attention from the family and medical staff. He really thought he was just in the hospital again. Soon, however, Michael had to go home. That marked the first night Daddy realized where he was. Gail and I were alone with him as we tried to leave him in the corridor. He ranted that he was going to call the police. He demanded a phone. He said we couldn't keep him there against his will, and he was right.

But we didn't phone the police. Instead, we got Michael on the phone. By then he was back in Florida. "Now, Daddy," Michael reasoned with him, "you know Mama can't do this alone at home. You've got to have help, so I need for you to do this for her. Promise me." Daddy sniffed nervously as he agreed to do as Michael said.

But as soon as he had handed the nurse the phone, he began to rant again and Gail and I simply left in tears. We felt perhaps the greatest moment of disloyalty ever in our lives.

I'll never forget the sound of my father's voice as he railed. His words echoed down the hall and perhaps haunt me to this day. "You aint gone put me out in some nursing home to die. You let me die here and I'll hont you. I'll hont ever damn one of you."

His resistance fueled his will to live. If only I could have understood that, then perhaps the process would not have been so draining.

Joe Lee complained to everyone who came into his room at the nursing home.

"Susie and Michael put me here," he'd tell his sisters. They commiserated. What a shame that poor Joe had to be in such a place.

"Just four walls. And not a drop of fresh coffee. People hollerin' out for 'mama' dern near all the time. If you aint lost your mind yet, you will."

My efforts to appease Daddy went unnoticed. "Do this for us, Daddy. Think of Lois." He complained about the food, about the crippled men and women who couldn't stay awake long enough to eat their supper. He griped about assigned seating at the dinner table, and he especially disliked Miss Golden.

"She aint a lady," Daddy would point as I sat with him in the dining room.

"Shut your damn mouth," she told Daddy. "He's a mean-ass man," she told me. To prove both points, the two often butted their wheelchairs and refused to budge.

"Get the hell out of my way," Daddy warned.

Finally, the nurses intervened.

He made fun of his numerous roommates who had to wear diapers. Mama's daily visits produced a predictable strain of complaints, to which she listened faithfully.

"It's just awful," she told me. "His hollerin' and their hollerin' and he blames you and I tell him, 'I caint do a thing about it, Joe.' But he won't listen. He's got that phone in his room and he calls me all in the night to come and get him out. And I just don't know how much more of this I can stand."

My advice was always short. "Hang up on him, Mama. Walk out. We'll take out the phone."

We did. Michael and Wayne were hurt because they had lost their direct connection to Daddy. They couldn't see him as we did, and the last link had been their phone calls. Was there no way to keep Daddy from calling Mama in the middle of the night? They wanted to know, and even though I explained, no one could really understand. The emotional loss was just too great.

Mama became a liberator again in her new role visiting residents at the nursing home. Each day she pranced through the dining area, pausing briefly to speak to everyone in lift seats or wheel chairs.

"And how are you today, Miss Alice?" she almost sang. "They just want somebody to touch'em and listen," Mama told me. She rarely stayed long enough to listen. Instead, in a burst of sudden energy, she would throw up her hands and exclaim, "Okay, now we need to liven up this old dead place!" When she played the piano, she could make even "Amazing Grace" sound like a ragtime dance.

"Praise the Lord, dammit," laughed Miss Golden. "Your mama can make the pianner sang!" Wheelchair bound, unable to breathe, Miss Golden would spring up, dance thirty seconds, collapse, and call for a breathing treatment.

Mama enjoyed her new mission. Each month's calendar featured "Sing-Along with Lois" on Wednesday afternoons.

The whole place would be rocking with "Victory in Jesus." Sometimes Daddy would join in. In time he preferred to stay in his room. "Tired today. Gotta get a little nap." Sometimes he would motion, "Sssh," when we tried to talk to him. "Don't wake up Lois." She took him the *Montgomery Advertiser* each day until he no longer read. She insisted on washing his clothes, although she complained of the odor. And she watched him decline, reporting each change.

"Joe's going downhill fast," she said. "What are we going to do, Susie?"

"We'll do what's next, Mama," I said, having no clue as to what that really might be.

"Don't ever do that to me," she entreated. "Don't put me in a nursing home. Don't let me live like that. I'd rather die."

"I won't, Mama."

"Don't ever do it, not to me, Susie. Let me die in the yard or sweeping leaves off the roof."

"I promise, Mama," I said. "Don't you have any faith?" What I couldn't tell her was that I was really having a hard time being strong, assuring everyone about matters that really were too much out of my control.

But Mama found a window of freedom, much more than I. I remember our seventeen-day trip out West. In each new town we reached, I called home. Mama told me to relax, that she and Daddy would be fine. But all I could think about was being too far away to reach them if they needed me. By the time we reached the apex of the mountain and our journey, I crouched down, crumbling by the weight of my burden. I looked across the twenty-mile Grand Canyon that looked like a three-dimensional postcard, and wept. Daddy had always wanted to go out West. "I'll pay for all of it," he had promised. "Y'all just take off work a couple weeks and we'll hit the trail, yeah, Buddy." But we had remembered the trip to Disney World when Daddy had talked ten hours straight, when each of us had taken turns listening to him. We couldn't imagine an almost infinite trek, but we had made it anyway, and Daddy was very much with me. I guess I should have known then that my father could never leave me, that even when he wasn't there, his spirit and voice were.

Unlike me, Mama seemed to find freedom from Daddy in her daily routines. As she had at the lake, she enjoyed staying awake past midnight, watching late movies with her little dogs and piping cockatoos. She seemed to revel in her newfound privacy. In the daytime, she stopped in at the nursing home only briefly and learned to not stay hours for lunch or Daddy's harassment. Instead, she roamed Dollar General, Fred's, and Wall-Mart freely.

And so in the four years that my father was in the nursing home, Mama found some personal freedom. It was not the freedom she imagined in her earlier years, but it was the space she craved. By eight p.m., if I had not called her first, Mama would call me.

"Just checking in," she always said with a slight laughing cough. Our informal agreement became routine, but its regularity gave her freedom with secure boundaries. In her new geriatric adolescence, she enjoyed pushing the limits by breaking the rules and keeping secrets.

"Don't tell Susie," she would make Dwan promise. "I'm going all the way to Wetumpka.

"I won't," he said, watching my mother peel curbs as her tires screeched. The yellow sticker on the back windshield of her 1986 Cutlass warned, "Grandma driving – may be hazardous to your health."

"That's an understatement," Dwan said, chuckling. Mama swore that if she couldn't drive, she wouldn't want to live. He shook his head as Mama swerved, narrowly missing assuming young boys on skate boards.

By then, Mama was almost eighty years old. "Sebendy-nine 'n holdin'," she liked to say.

"Slow down and wear your seat belt," I warned.

"Don't you have any faith, Susie?" she'd yell out the window as she headed out for Kmart at dusk. "If I get lost in the parking lot, I know how to call you!"

Never mind that Mama couldn't see at all. "I see enough," she said, smiling. Dwan would wave, then motion to me. "Let'er go – you can't stop her. Lord sure looks out for her – and everybody else."

Still, there were the facts from which no one could escape; even Mama with her daily escapades. From time to time, she called Hazel when residents at the nursing home complained that my father kept everyone awake. "He calls my name all night. Nobody can sleep," she complained. "And he's just so loud. You can hear him as soon as you walk in the front door."

"It's just because he loves you, Lois. He absolutely adores you, always has. He don't mean nothing by it," Hazel reassured her. She could comfort Mama unlike anyone else.

# XXV

## Obituaries

If you listen to what the elderly don't say, you can see that survival becomes cruel. The daily list of obituaries, the perfunctory calls from a cousin or church member, a routine list like grocery shopping once was, so comes the news that someone else, perhaps once close, has died. And so the elderly take the news like they do their daily heart medicine or blood pressure pill.

They learn to distance themselves, wrap the news with silence. And they survive.

For several years, I had been my parents' chaperone, escorting them to funerals or doctors' visits, often on the same day. At funerals, they sometimes saw the aged faces of once familiar acquaintances. Sometimes they had to be introduced. Little by little, the circle dissolved, the aunts, the uncles, the Millbrook Singers. My parents had become – like so many of the elderly isolated in their homes or in nursing homes – sole survivors. Friends were memories, fading, past, deceased.

After a while, when there was little consolation found, few people found at the funerals to console, my parents only read the obituaries. It was enough. They would send me instead of going themselves, or I would think I had to go.

Sometimes, a sense of duty, responsibility, I would attend the funerals alone, the family delegate introducing myself as "Joe and Lois's daughter." Someone would still know them, someone would still faintly remember. And then they would make the connection.

"You know, Joe and Lois– he worked on the railroad and she played the pianner. An' you – you played too, didn't you? Are you still playin' the pianner? Why, I remember when you was just a little thing..."

Gail didn't go to funerals, not for Mama and Daddy, not to help me. "I just can't take it," she said. "I don't need to be the family delegate."

"I don't blame you," I said, but at the time I did.

At the nursing home, news of another death ushered in a day of silence. Patients would simply stay in their rooms for the day. That's how commonplace death had become.

But when the news came of Hazel Liveoak's disappearance, there was nothing ordinary or commonplace about it.

The screams through Mama's cries could not diminish the words of anguish. All Mama could say was, "Oh, Hazel, Hazel, Hazel. Not Hazel."

For three days we had watched the surrealistic television coverage. She had been abducted from the Food World parking lot in the most visible time of day, three o'clock p.m. Family members told us Mrs. Liveoak had gone to the store to buy a cake mix on her sister's birthday. Her church directory picture, the insurance photo of her car, the modest home in which she had always lived in Millbrook, Alabama, all were shown on television, as though we were watching *Unsolved Mysteries*.

And on the third day, both her car and Hazel were found in yet another parking lot, again in the exposed light of day. In the trunk was the lifeless body of the woman who'd been my mother's ally for fifty years. She had died of a heart attack.

Later I would think of the cruel irony, how Hazel, Mama, and Daddy – all had survived an endless round of heart repairs. And then, to simply be placed in a trunk in mid-July. To die. All for the meager amount of money Hazel had to offer two desperate people with a crack habit.

As Mama got the news, she literally wailed. This was not how things were supposed to happen. You weren't supposed to survive heart attacks and surgeries and live out the often desperate struggles of aging and see others die slowly, only to be abruptly, brutally, heartlessly killed because some desperate person needed drug money.

When I took Mama to the funeral home, I saw my friends from long ago, Hazel's girls and Larry, there now with their own children. I thought of our dancing long ago. What a contrast to the way they now held themselves together with silent, incomprehensible dignity. Mama's sobs were uncontrollable, so I escorted her out, promising that we would all get together soon. We had shared a common past, common parents. Now we were bound silently by the most extraordinary, uncommon event, the way things were never supposed to be.

"Did Larry tell you?" Mama asked me in the car. "They were in the backseat. The girl confessed. She told everything, how they took her to the ATM and took all her money. Hazel didn't have much. They could have let her go." Instead, they had taken her to the woods and tied her up, but she hadn't begged for her life. Instead, Mama said, she pleaded with them to ask Jesus for salvation. "Hazel did that," Mama said.

"No, no one told me," I said

If I could have taken away my mother's pain, oh, how I would done so. Instead, I held her like a child, cradled her in my arms as she wept. "Oh, Lord Jesus, Lord Jesus. Not Hazel, not Hazel."

As I silently mourned the loss of Mama's tree of life, Hazel Liveoak, I realized something about our lives had changed forever.

# XXVI

## Atonement

For over a year, Daddy fought the nursing home, fought Mama, fought the nurses who tried to help him. Mama sometimes railed that Daddy was still controlling her. He could still call all the shots and hurt – even though she had the power to leave and not listen.

Not only did he keep everyone awake by loudly calling out for Lois throughout the night, but also there were new, strange behaviors. When nurses were changing or bathing him, he would reach for their breasts. At other times he would openly call caretakers "damn niggers." With strokes and dementia came the erratic railing of a man near the end of his life. He showed no control, and his own abusive behavior led the nursing home director to call me. She said that if we weren't able to get him under control, he'd have to be sent to a state hospital. The nursing home had a code of conduct, and Daddy was breaking the rules.

Ashamed, Mama was in tears. "What are we going to do, Susie?" Mama cried repeatedly in her desperation.

"We'll do what's next," I said. I had no idea what that really meant now. Suddenly, I found myself in the unfathomable position of being responsible for and defending the man who had been the leader of his own family for nearly sixty years. My daddy, my own father. Just to get through the tough situations, as I had so many times before, I promised myself that I would just have a good cry later.

I dismissed Daddy's lack of self-control as the result of stroke and dementia, but Mama could see nothing but shame and embarrassment. Often, his loud denigration would turn into tirades for all the world to see and hear. He berated her so much that Mama was spiritually, emotionally stripped. I told Daddy that he if he didn't behave himself, he would have to be locked up in a state facility. But Daddy could understand no consequences for his behavior. "I'm already in prison," he maintained.

Finally, I called my pastor and told him the struggles Mama was undergoing because of Daddy's lack of self-control. All of us had exhausted any hope of pacifying him or altering his actions.

"He's mean to everyone," I told Henry Smith. "He is sexually explicit, angry, miserable – and bringing grief to everyone around him," I confessed. What I couldn't tell him was that I was hurting too, that I felt Mama's agony as much as Daddy's. That I too felt shame and responsibility for Daddy's misconduct. Sometimes I would wake in the night, sit straight up in bed and call out for Daddy or Mama. As I realized that I had been thinking of someone or something besides my parents, especially Daddy, I gasped. Their own agony had become my obsession. But I couldn't tell Henry these selfish thoughts.

Instead, I told him about Daddy's anger, the constant berating, and most of all, his endless pain, his shoulders, his knees broken, his heart torn apart. Our own hearts were torn apart, too. And Mama's desperation; she felt so helpless, so publicly shamed.

So at this most dire moment of ours lives, I asked Henry to pray. He visited Daddy, as he had so many times before, sometimes giving communion, sometimes not. He prayed with Daddy and for Daddy, asked him, said, "Joe, I know that you love Lois. Now I just want you to call upon the Lord to soften your heart, so that you can be the Lord's servant and witness even when it isn't easy." The simplicity of a godly man's words is a healing memory, even now.

In a lucid moment, Daddy must have felt the call of the Holy Spirit, proffered through the gentle prayers of a faithful servant. A man like Henry can do that with just so few words – bring faith, hope, assurance. All gain incandescence in his wake.

Henry told me of his private meeting with Daddy, how he'd asked Joe to pray with him but that he wouldn't. He simply said "all right" and bowed his head as Henry prayed.

When I arrived Saturday to visit and give Mama a respite, I found Daddy slumped over in his wheelchair. He had soiled his clothes and fallen asleep, completely unaware. At first I was alarmed.

"Daddy, Daddy, what's wrong?" I nudged his arm gently, aware that his calcified shoulders could so easily hurt. A string of drool streamed down his chin, and I wiped it with my sleeve as I tried to awaken him. He tried to open his eyes, but he was listless, somnolent, so incoherent that I was sure he had been drugged, or worse.

And I felt the fear I had so many times before, the kind that paralyzes from the feet to the heart, the fear that he'd had another stroke.

I called for a nurse, but it was Abigail, a day-shift aide, who met me in the hall, hugging me, reassuring. "It's the Lawd's doin', don't you worry none," she consoled me.

Our prayers had been answered in a way we never dreamed.

The doctors wanted to conduct tests to see what part of Daddy's brain had been damaged by the latest episodes, but my heart knew the answer that no scan could fathom. I looked to Abigail and the heavens, and called my brothers while I consoled my mother. My brothers agreed: tests weren't necessary, and the time had arrived to simply give Daddy his peace. Abigail had been right.

When Mama arrived each day, she found a different man.

There would be no more shouting, blaming, berating. A week earlier Daddy had threatened to call the police if someone didn't get him out of the nursing home, but now? Now he didn't even know what day it was, much less where he was.

What was left was not the Joe Lee anyone had known. He was complacent, content, and almost totally unaware of his surroundings. It was not a resolution anyone could have foreseen, but it was an answer all the same. And I got down on my knees, alone in my room, and prayed, "Thank you, Lord. Thank you for giving Daddy peace."

But my heart cried that silent prayer of longing – because I missed my daddy. He was in God's hands now, not mine, and I missed him so.

Something about our lives changed forever.

Bereft of self-dignity, Daddy would wait patiently and without complaint until someone noticed that he had soiled his clothing, indeed the very bed in which he spent most of his last three years in the nursing home. Most times when either Mama or I arrived, it was one of us who summoned help. Daddy didn't really care, nor did he notice those around him. He knew only Abigail by name. He called to her as his own daughter.

"Oh, Abigail," he would almost sing. "How 'bout a lit'l coffee, Abigail?"

"Your father is a happy man, aint he?" Abigail always told me. "But he gets on these kicks. He just won't be satisfied – he say he got to talk to Fred? Who's Fred?" she asked me.

"Fred is his brother, but he died a decade ago."

"Well, I found the s'lution already," said Abigail. "When I couldn't get you on the phone, I call my brother and I say 'I needs you to do me a little favor. Mistah Lee need to talk to Fred.' And my brother say, 'put him on the phone.' And you know, I put Mistah Lee on that tel-ee-phone and he talk to my brother thirty minutes the other night. He dint know no better. But he do feel better."

Abigail laughed. I cried as I hugged her.

And when Daddy had to go to the oral surgeon, Abigail

went too, lifting Daddy, wheeling him, ensuring his broken knee and calcified shoulders weren't mishandled. Abbie alone could take Daddy through the ritual of being changed or moved without any pain.

"Okay, Mistah Lee, now grab holt to me right here. We're going up," she'd say as she picked him up like a baby.

"Now lean on me, Mistah Lee."

"All right, Abigail. You're the boss," Daddy would say.

Always conscientious about hygiene, the man now in my father's body could no more brush his teeth than he could tie his shoes. His teeth simply had decayed; four at one time would have to be removed surgically.

In the waiting room at the oral surgeon's office, Abigail and I drank coffee and shared our views of life, found common ground.

"You really go beyond the call of duty," I told her.

"You gotta love these old people," she said. "I love'em like they was my own. That's why I been here fourteen years. Aint nobody else here been doing this as long as I have 'cept Mizz Golden. She say she spent her whole life in the nursin' home, first workin', now living–"

"You gotta love'em," I agreed. Then I looked at her, remembering my father's own words from a decade earlier. I couldn't voice the words, but I remembered how my father had turned to me on the elevator after seeing Moses for the last time, how he had said, "I think race relations are better now than they have ever been in this country." But I couldn't bring myself to share the memory with Abigail or tell her that she was a sister to me.

My mother was insistent that the weekend Stephanie was to be married, Pop was not to attend.

"Under no circumstances. Do you hear me?" she told Michael. She knew how Daddy's incontinence could be disastrous, how he'd drool, fall asleep sitting up and literally plunge from his wheelchair.

"No way," she said. She threw her hands up when Michael refused to concede. "Call Susie. She's in charge. It's her day, not mine."

Michael's wife of thirty years had been divinely appointed. Of this I am sure. She found Pop's dress shirts. She purchased dress socks and slip-on shoes at Kmart. The swelling in his feet made wearing his wing tips impossible; they were still in the top of his closet, as though he would get well and come home, still polished from the last singing I'd taken him to at Maple Springs.

Abigail dressed Pop. When no one else could, she put on Daddy's undershirt even though he couldn't lift his arms. She padded him with layers of Depends. She put on his pants and shirt and tied his shoes – all so that he could attend the wedding of his granddaughter. "You're going to a wedding, Mr. Lee," she said. By then Michael and Sandra had arrived with the freshly cleaned wheelchair.

"Daddy, we're going to a wedding. Are you ready?" the couple smiled together.

"Sho nuff?" said Daddy. "Whose wedding, Susie's?"

"Naw, naw – her daughter's," Michael clarified.

And they stuffed him into the wheelchair, pulled up to the church, and rolled out Daddy. "Curb service," he smiled.

For an hour he played the role well. When Stephanie saw her grandfather in the center of the church fellowship hall, the first tears of the day, her hands covering her face, the magic of a Christmas morning – all were revealed in an instant.

Pop celebrated that day, holding his punch cup high and exclaiming to perfect strangers, "Why, I declare. I haven't seen you in twenty years!"

At other times, he rightly recognized people he really had

known and recalled the exact details of their last meeting.

It was uncanny. But soon he was tired. Michael and Sandra secretly wheeled him away as Gail laughed, "Uh-oh, meter's up." As I watched the couple roll my father out the back ramp, even at the height of the celebration, a sadness filmed over my mixed tears. "He looks like George Wallace," I said to myself. "And he'll never know it."

After the wedding, we drank wine and beer for the first time in at least twenty years. In our piano room, we sang Mama's version of "Will the Circle Be Unbroken?" Later, Allison moved the Queen Anne chairs so all could dance as she sang "Let'er Rip." Admittedly, I played a little boogie on the piano, and Allison impatiently beat out the tempo for me to follow. "C'mon, Mama – you need a little rhythm here," she said.

# Ecclesiastes 3: 1-8

To every thing there is a season, and a time to every purpose under the
      heaven;
A time to be born, and a time to die;
A time to plant, and a time to pluck up that which is planted;
A time to kill, and a time to heal; a time to break down, and a time to
      build up;
A time to weep, and a time to laugh;
A time to mourn, and a time to dance;
A time to cast away stones, and a time to gather stones together;
A time to embrace, and a time to refrain from embracing;
A time to get, and a time to lose;
A time to keep, and a time to cast away;
A time to rend, and a time to sew;
A time to keep silence, and a time to speak;
A time to love, and a time to hate;
A time of war,
And a time of peace.

# XXVII
## Comfort

There is no natural light in an emergency room where the time of day or night is canceled by the flood of invasive fluorescence. When I got the three a.m. call from the nursing home that my father was going to the hospital by ambulance, I left without telling anyone, even Mama. Daddy couldn't breathe, and the sounds of his moaning and painful writhing could be heard even in the hospital lobby. For an hour, I tried to reassure him, holding his hand to let him know I was there.

"Lois, Lois," he called. "Oh, Lois."

He took no comfort in my presence. The doctors soon told me Daddy was in septic shock, that his kidneys and heart were failing.

"Oh, Lois, Lois," he called out.

And so I called my mother as calmly as I could. In the background, her little dogs barked.

"Put on your clothes – have a cup of coffee. But I'm afraid I'm going to have to come get you, Mama," I said.

With a dampened wash cloth, Mama bathed Daddy's head.

"You'll be all right, Joe, everything's going to be all right."

For the first time, Daddy opened his eyes to follow the sound of her voice as she reassured him.

"You're going to a better place, no more pain. You'll be free. Don't be afraid. I'll be with you."

The touch of her voice brought him the only peace he had in the darkness of that morning. And he trusted her, only her. She knew then that it would not be long. For the next three days, she walked the halls of the small-town hospital, tossing flowers from a basket, singing softly, consoling family, comforting strangers, thanking nurses.

"Don't you have any faith, Susie? Don't you see?" she asked.

I prayed that Daddy would not die before the rest of the family could see him, that he wouldn't die on Mama's birthday. The next day, he was conscious enough to eat Jello. When I told him it was Mama's birthday, he declared, rather weakly, "I'll have to take her out."

"What, what did he say?" I asked the nurse as she spoon-fed Daddy.

"He said he'll have to take her out." We laughed, and Daddy smiled faintly. I prayed that he wouldn't die when I was alone with him. And he waited. He waited because he had to, until anyone who wished to see him could do so.

In the small hospital, the staff didn't make me wait for the official visiting hours in the intensive care unit. Instead, I stayed with Daddy all day and throughout much of the night. When Michael arrived, he did the same. Daddy livened up from all the company and attention. The nurses, Michael, and I kept him clean and comfortable. Carefully, Michael shaved Daddy and insisted on finding Daddy's favorite aftershave lotion.

"Old Spice and everything nice," Michael said as he smoothed the covers for our father. I couldn't help thinking how relieved Daddy must be to be bathed daily instead of twice a week, to have his family dote over his every move. "Boy, hi-dee," I still can hear him say. His dignity had been restored. It was good enough for Daddy.

As the antibiotics fought the staff infection that had invaded all of his vital organs, Daddy began to feel better. Still, we stayed with him in the intensive care unit, Michael and I, one of us nearly all the time. Daddy liked that. How many times we had done this before, Michael and I couldn't say, and in so many ways, this time felt like any other hospitalization. The unspoken truth remained silent in our hearts. Michael remained perpetually optimistic, something I would later appreciate as a gift.

But my heart knew the truth to which I did not want to listen, knew my mother's gift of sensing the truth behind everything left unsaid. Still, the rest of us avoided talking about serious matters. Instead, we asked him if he needed his head propped a little more, or if was he ready for a little coffee.

The finality of the coming hours and days was unvoiced. Daddy never acknowledged that he knew or suspected a thing, and I couldn't help thinking that maybe this time, like all the others, he would defy death.

But as I brought the latest cup of coffee and slice of lemon meringue pie, Daddy looked right at me, as though he were completely and utterly cognizant and competent, and when no one else could hear him, he whispered, "I want you to look out after your little mama."

I swallowed the tears.

"You know I will, Daddy," I said. Then I smiled. "But you'll have to give me a dime."

Daddy chuckled. "All right, Li'l Chap. All right."

Abigail knew. She seemed to know when the time would come, and she insisted on visiting Daddy alone. The hours of his life were waning, and Abigail knew.

Her shameless wailing echoed throughout the intensive care unit, and I met her with open arms as she came out, not bothering to shut the door. We hugged and pleaded for God's mercy on Joe Lee. I prayed that Daddy would not know how much we grieved: I didn't want to frighten him.

Abigail held me and wouldn't let go. And in that moment, my heart was opened once again, humbled by the great equalizer of life, the realization that life is tenuous and shared, and ends.

"I sho gone-a miss'im," Abigail said. She spoke for me. For

the first time I acknowledged the truth that lay ahead, but there were no words through my tears. The first raw moments of grief take away our words, our power to do anything except hold tight to those who love and comfort us. She held me for what seemed like hours.

And when the final time came early on a Sunday morning, the Lord's Day, that great day of resurrection, the family gathered around Daddy's bed as the pastor asked us to hold hands and sing "Blessed Assurance." And the evening and the morning were the fulfillment of time, and we said goodbye to Daddy for the last time.

We went outside, unsure of what to do next, but sunshine filled us with a sense of quiet calm and peace. Time seemed to stop in the overwhelming tranquility of the Lord's Day as Michael cradled Mama in his arms for what seemed like hours.

"Sho gone-a miss'im."

Something about our lives had changed forever.

# XXVIII

## Forbidden Mourning

My mother spent exactly a week mourning the death of my father, her husband for fifty-eight years. Soon she entered one of the those phases you only read about – she became inconsolably angry, only her anger wasn't exactly the stage of grief one usually imagines follows the death of a spouse. She wasn't mad that she had been left alone. No, her anger was something far more complex. She was mad that my father had been the man he was, and I soon learned that the sheer definition of that was a source of contention. Mama was like the wild dog she had nursed back to health so many years ago. I couldn't go near her.

She was angry that I had written a tribute honoring Daddy and had published it in the local newspaper and had even made copies for the family. "Don't write anything else about Joe, and don't let anybody read it – not my family, not his. It's not true. He was not who you think he was." Mama spat accusations.

"He wasn't just a man to me, Mama – he was an era, my father."–

"He was no hero, Susie," she said.

"Mama, this will be different for everyone," I assured her. "I'm sorry you couldn't love Daddy without hating him, and I understand that, but he's dead, Mama, and a lot of people – including me, your own children, and your grandchildren – loved and really miss him, people who looked up to him."

"You didn't know him," she fired off. "He hurt so many people."

"Mama, what do you want us to do now? Say he was cruel to you, that you wasted fifty-eight years of your life? I can't say all that now, Mama. My father, your husband, my daughters' grandfather – this man is no longer on Earth with us. May God rest his soul – and yours." I had said too much. Dwan was better at this than I was, I thought – even Gail. Why couldn't someone else do the dirty work for a change? Even as I thought these things, I knew Mama could see through my self-pity, but she didn't seem to be listening.

So I decided to keep my thoughts to myself, and I watched helplessly as Mama spun out of control. She called her sister to validate what a cruel man my father had been. She thought everyone should understand her bitterness. I told my mother there were certain aspects of life and death that I couldn't help her with, and I offered to help her find a counselor, a pastor, anyone besides me. But I too had reached a turning point. There was nothing more I could do for my mother other than to offer to take her shopping, to cook for her, to take her relentlessly, it seemed, to the doctor and to emergency rooms. Her breathing problems became the very symbol of her inability to swallow the truth that had been her life.

In the year that followed, I felt helpless as Mama sorted through the memories that haunted her. She refused to eat, and after two trips to the emergency room in the first month after Daddy's death, I lost count. By spring, she had heart failure, and her hospital stay turned into weeks. I prayed for her to find peace. I prayed that she wouldn't die so soon, and she waited, as she always could. She waited because she had to. Still, my heart felt a connection I could not verbalize in so many words.

"She won't make it a year," I quietly told my daughters. We hoped that I was wrong. But in the private universe of mothers and daughters, they too knew too much. How many times I had hoped that I would not involve my own daughters emotionally like my mother had, but even that seemed another struggle I could not win.

# XXIX

## Promises Fulfilled

She had been too stubborn to call for help that day, the eve of the now infamous 9/11, the last normal day for so many Americans. Later we found notes she'd left on the table, just how many Lasix she had taken, the number of Tylenol, everything but an explanation about why she had not phoned for help in time. And so the only call she made late that day was to 911. Her only message to the emergency respondents, "Heart," or so the paramedics told me at the hospital.

It had been her last sole word uttered in quiet desperation. Later I would appreciate the symbol, but in the days that followed, I couldn't find any words.

Thankfully, Mama would never know the terror that halted the entire world the following morning.

The only sound in the small intensive care unit was the rhythm of the breathing machine, and to divert the agony inside as I watched the lifeless form of my mother, I went to the waiting room to watch television. As the second plane flew into the World Trade Center, a silent crew of nurses came into the room. They gripped their faces in disbelief. Some wanted to get their children from school. Others made phone calls in panic. I watched silently and exchanged assurances with a nurse whose son I taught. She promised me that Mama was having the best care and that she was in no pain. None of the events seemed real to me; it was as though I were in some surrealistic video, and the explosions on television matched my inner turmoil. From the window at the end of the hospital corridor, I could see cars lined up at the gas station across the street as panic spread. It was like the whole world was listening and knew fear. Allison and Stephanie took turns going with me into the intensive care unit.

"This is what the end of the world must be like," I told Allison, who had just turned eighteen. "A traffic jam, being stuck where you can't get out and don't know where to go. It's like a parallel universe." I tried to assure my daughters that no matter what, we would be okay.

And the morning and the evening were the first day, and we tried not to be afraid. In the hospital's front lobby, an elderly woman wearing oxygen tubes and carting a tank confided in me.

"This is like the day the Nazis took Holland," she said with an accent. "My father hid Jews. I was just eight." She had driven to the hospital to feel safe. She was afraid of bombing, of being alone in war. She was that eight-year-old again, torn from her parents and her home.

And so I listened and reassured the new friend, whose name I soon learned. Anne had lost her husband months ago, much like my own mother had. Since then, she had often returned to find refuge in the hospital lobby. Before long, we had connected a mutual friend, my church pastor.

"He has a Dutch bible," you know, said Anne, "but his Dutch is horrible. Don't tell Henry I said so," she finally laughed. We prayed the twenty-third Psalm together, and she gripped my hands in tears, thanking me.

I had no flowers to toss from a basket that day, but the sense that one has always a mission at an appointed place in time gave me focus and peace.

And on the third day, I silently gave the nurses Mama's living will. My daughters stayed with me all week. Allison said that she was okay as long as she was near me, but she could not bear to be around people at school. There, everyone was in a state of shock and the normal routine had been replaced by fear that the world was going to end. Classes were interrupted for prayer assemblies. I knew exactly what she meant, although I tried to disagree.

Gail came in and left periodically. Finally, Michael arrived on Thursday. He had been unable to leave because of the national defense emergency and the lockdown at the base where he worked.

He verbalized about so many missed medical queues and described the ideal scenario for Mama's recovery. I wanted to believe him, but something inside reminded me of that secret universe between mothers and daughters, and so I knew.

"I don't think it's going to happen," I told him. "This is exactly what Mama did not want. She made me promise, Michael."

"Susie, she's our Mama too. You've just got to be in control," Gail intervened. I went back to the lobby, hoping to see my Dutch friend.

And so we waited, and I said nothing while Michael talked to Wayne by cell phone. Wayne had told me, as so often before, that he was not coming home unless he had to. I wondered what that really meant and was angry. It would be months before I really understood that everyone has a different way of dealing with grief, that no one way is the right way.

I waited and waited and prayed for God's mercy. I could almost hear my mother say, "Susie, don't you have any faith?" And she held out, as she always could. She waited because she had to.

And when the time had been fulfilled, the doctors removed the tubes and turned off the breathing machine that had given the family a last chance. My sister sneaked in Iddy Biddy, Mama's smallest Yorkie. The dog quietly licked Mama's face, overjoyed to see her. Mama's eyelids fluttered, the first sign of response in so many days. When she breathed on her own for several hours, it seemed as though the miraculous might occur. Then her breathing became erratic.

Gail gripped Mama's hands and pleaded with her to stay. "Don't go, Mama, we need you," she said through her sobs.

I tried to be brave, to say what I thought I should rather than

what I felt. "It's okay, Mama. You'll be all right. We'll be all right."
And I stood back. "Let'er go," I said. "Let'er go."

The final moments of her life were without struggle. She opened her eyes, looked beyond consciousness, and simply stopped. The chaos of the world's turmoil had ended the week in the peace of life's most  private moment.

# XXX

## Going Home

The day after we buried Mama, Michael and I went back to the grave site to say goodbye in the solitude of our grief. The day should have been cloudy, I thought. Only raging thunderstorms and sudden hail storms could match our grief.

Instead, a thousand yellow monarchs as light as the Indian summer sky laced our parents' graves. And I lay down upon the wreaths that covered the graves where the butterflies danced and our parents lay silent, and there, we wept and gave them up.

Something about our lives had changed forever.

Nothing prepares a person for the finality of death or the duties and anger which follow, the seemingly simple matters that feed the grief almost on a daily basis – opening the mail, hearing the phone ring, hearing my mother's voice on the answering machine. Feeding her dogs and making promises I can't keep.

When I faced my mother's bedroom, I half expected to find her there, napping with her Yorkie who now wagged his tail and barked in anticipation. He thought I would bring her home this time, and he paced the hall, knowing she was just behind me and that everything would be the way it was before.

In my parents' home, Granny's mantel clock kept time, a cruel irony in the wake of death. On the back porch, Mama's birds still sang and talked, waiting for her to come outside and let them out of their cages. Pretty Boy didn't understand why he couldn't perch on Lois's shoulder. He whistled at me, once, then again, and again, and again, "I'm a pretty boy! I'm a pretty boy. Whii–wheewwww!" he sang.

"Mama's gone," I said. And then there were tears. There

would be hours of tears. Days and nights and weeks of a loss like none I'd ever known. A dark pit. Sometimes I couldn't breathe.

I see your picture there on the piano, Daddy – forever twenty-nine and young, the world at your door, your twenty-one-year-old wife alive and forever yours, untainted by the pain to come. Before children, before time, before the grips of responsibility and words.

Songbooks still clipped open on the piano, and, oh, how I loved to hear you sing, the two of you. And you'd say, "Play me a little tune, Susie."

If only I could play forever, keep this forever, never go home – because in a way I will never leave, just as you, always, always in my heart and mind will never leave me alone or unmindful or ungrateful. My new creed: that I will never forget.

Gail can't come home yet. She says she can't take it. In some ways, neither can I – but here I am again, doing the duties of life and death as before. I want to throw up my hands and scream and tell everyone how unfair this is – how I feel like an only child and I'm angry inside, how I miss Mama and you, and how in my heart Mama was never old, how I wanted to fix things for her and never gave up. How I made promises to her, to you, Daddy, private promises, those from the heart.

And how I'd love to run and run and run until I got home, far, far away, how I want God to take away this pain, this memory, this echo from the bottom of my heart that just cries, "Mama, not Mama, Lord Jesus, not Mama." I want to say, "It's Gail's turn," but I can't. In some ways, the cold war never ends.

For someone, afer all, has to do the part – pay the bills for the deceased, notify Social Security and Railroad Retirement, send out death certificates, another paradox, surely; cancel credit cards and newspapers and handle the cruel ironies of life after death. Someone has to wash the clothes for the last time and clean out the refrigerator. It's what Gail calls the rubble; what's left. Even in her grief, she has a sense of humor. You'd like that.

Still, how glad I am, Daddy, that you didn't live to see this part. It's just too hard. You could not have taken it, just like all those times Mama was in the hospital; you couldn't take that either. So here I am again, and I will go on because I have to, as you did, as Mama did. Someday, I'll tell my children and grandchildren the whole story.

How I cleaned through my tears until I became nauseous and ran home, to my home, screaming. I would come again another day. And I did, thinking it would get easier. It didn't get any easier. I realized I couldn't do it alone, this hard part.

And so Dwan came back with me. He is better at this than I am or can ever be. He held the garbage bags. Someone must clean up in the life after death. Someone has to decide what to throw out or keep.

And I kept waiting, wanting all of it to be instantly behind me, finished, resolved. I phoned Gail, but she wasn't ready to face the chores or memories that remained.

"Just take care of Susie," she said. She was insistent that nothing really had to be finished yet, that the time hadn't arrived. I told her she didn't understand. She said she understood more than I knew, and the silence that followed was more revealing than any before. For the first time, I thought maybe she was right all along.

"They're still using you, Susie. You just don't get it," she said. Abandoned, confused, I had been here before, alone, and so I said nothing. I had to work alone through the pain and anger until I finally understood.

And so I've written this, knowing you will hear me, and forgive, even as I have looked, found, cried, and forgiven.

Grief and redemption are equally solitary.

But there would be another revelation. As I closed the front door to your home, I saw it there on the front mat, shining in the mid-day sun, a dime.

Perhaps for the first time, I smiled as I picked it up and looked toward the heavens where surely you were looking down with a grin.

"You win, Daddy. You win," I conceded.

And as I inspected the dime, through tears and smiles, I knew of the miracle, and I could almost hear you say, "All right, Li'l Chap. All right."

Spinning the dime before I pocketed it forever, I made this last promise: I promise to remember you in thanksgiving for all we experienced, endured, embraced, and survived – and that, and that even when I am afraid, I will find enough faith and courage to sustain me, no matter who's listening.

Now I can close the door and go home again, for what I found was more than remained.

I took the dime.

# Epilogue
## Peace

This rock is not mine, I remind myself. The massive limestone rock on which I sit belongs to so many before me, and I have sat here now for hours, meditating without words or even complete thoughts, looking at the Coosa River and wondering about how anyone could have ever taken the land from the Alabama Indians. I think about Granny and her Creek grandparent. Some day, I think, I'll find out the Indian name of that grandparent, but even that doesn't really matter anymore. The legacy is enough.

For six months I have avoided the graveyard where my parents are buried in Slapout, Alabama. It is enough to put silk flowers there a few times a year. Mama never wanted to see real flowers wasted on a grave site.

Instead, Dwan and I spend our spare time stepping off the distance from the front of the planned house to its back in the wooded acres on our land by the lake. We are careful not to get too heady about the prospects of this land we've just bought. If we speak too loudly or boastfully or knowingly, we might jeopardize the chance that someday, hopefully soon, we'll be able to look up from our table and see only tall hickories and the gentle slope of the hill as it feeds the shallows of the Coosa.

And so we joke about putting up a tent here by the water, and that too would be okay. Somehow, it is enough just to be here, to have made the circle, to have found the River Jordan, as I used to tell Mama. If only Mama had lived to see this land, but then, we might not be here if she had lived. And I think of how life changes, yet so little changes. The water still – always – leads home.

Surrounded by hundred-year-old white oaks and beechwood, I am content to name none in honor of a friend or loved one. The rustling of leaves on the hillside is enough, and the peaceful presence of memories never haunts me, though I'm always listening.

Here on the Coosa I can imagine what De Soto must have seen in his historic trek through Elmore County. And when I look across the river to the woods on the other side, why, it seems like time just has no boundary, like this is where I have been and belonged all along. Children grown, but one day they too will bring their children, just as I brought mine to the water. And we will marvel at the rocks beside the river and dig for worms in the dark, moist soil by the water. We may go out in the boat, or we may just sit here by the water and bait our cane poles. We'll wait for something to bite, and when we don't get any bites, we'll wait some more. And that will be good enough.

One day, one day we'll float down the Alabama all the way to the Mobile River and maybe even the Gulf. That's what Dwan has always wanted to do. But as I look across the Coosa here in Elmore County, and I look down as far as I can see, I think maybe we've already been down that river, and this is just as good a place as any. It is enough.

Beside the still waters of our small inlet, a deer trail looks as though it's been walked for years. So I take that path to the water, and sometimes I look up, and sometimes I look across. Sometimes, not often, I think about how my parents' home was just five miles downriver near the Jordan Dam. But this is enough. When you walk down by the river and look across the small slough, you can't see it, but you can hear a waterfall nearby. It's underneath the willow trees that cover the bank. Just beyond the waterfall is a mammoth-sized rock, and near the top, where several rocks join together, as surely they did a million years ago, an unseen child has placed an American flag.

I can just imagine a ten- or twelve-year-old claiming the Coosa

River and proudly climbing that rock to post the flag. Sometimes I imagine I am that child. Other times I think about how my grandchildren will climb that rock, and we'll sit out here by the river. Maybe I'll look back up the bank, into the trees, and tell them stories about their grandparents, how their great-grandmother Lee was like a  pioneer, a pioneer woman of great, often silent courage, and their great-grandfather, Joe Lee, why he was a railroader during steam engine days, and he was a storyteller. If he didn't know a good story, why, he'd make it up, my mother used to say.

And their great-great-grandmother, Granny Countryman? She was a quarter Creek Indian, or so she claimed, and lived in the crossroads of Owassa, which I think must mean that place by the river where the water branches. She's buried there, Mount Olive at Owassa,  as a matter of fact – the birthplace of my mother.

We're all connected, I'll tell them. And maybe my grandchildren will see me rock on a porch, rock, rock, rock, and know that silence sometimes says what you can't.

And when my grandchildren ask me about growing up, I'll tell them that growing up in the 1960's was a time of great change in Alabama. I'll tell them about George Wallace and their great grandfather and how in some ways they were alike. I'll tell them about breaking down the barriers of injustice and prejudice, maybe, and what the cold war was really all about in Alabama, how life and time and the Lord – all have a way of changing you when you aren't looking. My grandchildren likely won't understand, but I'll rock, and maybe I'll tell them how I climbed and fell out of a pine tree and carried a branch in my leg all the way home without crying.

I'll tell them about gospel singings where the men sat on one side of the country church and the women folk, why they sat on the other, and from all over the countryside, wherever we went, you could feel the beat of the music as a hundred people patted their feet. I'll tell them about Ebbie Barrington announcing the Millbrook Singers, "And playin' for us today is Li'l Susie. She's just ten years old," and how I stayed ten until I was thirteen and embarrassed. And we'll laugh. And I'll tell them about Gail, some at least, how she just thought she could outrun me.

And I'll tell them how their great-grandmother Lois stood up for women's rights before it was even popular, about Hortense Peel and the Vacation Bible School parade through Millbrook, Alabama. They'll get a kick out of that. When you ride across Alabama, you can still find small towns like that, I'll tell them. Some of them are so unchanged, even though Daddy was right about the passenger trains.

I'll tell them about the sound of the train, how their great-grandfather rode steam engines and worked mighty hard. Then I'll look out across the water and tell them about Pop. "There's good and bad in everybody," I'll say. And I'll stop, because there's no need to tell little children more than they need to hear. They'll understand, by and by.

Maybe I'll tell them that the point of it all, as Joe Lee would say, is that you have to look life square in the eye, like you were looking right at a train and knew when to move. And how you can't be afraid. Maybe I'll tell them what a dime was worth when I was growing up. Maybe I'll tell them how I learned there was life after death. Maybe they'll understand. In time they will.

Maybe I'll be able to play a few tunes on the piano for my grandchildren, or maybe I'll just pretend I can't play and show them the black notes. "One day," I'll promise them, "you'll learn how to play all the keys, even the black notes." In my heart, I know they will know the tune, no matter what key. Shaped notes, round, words or not – we're all of the same melody and making, I'll tell them. Maybe they'll listen. They'll understand, by and by.

And maybe we'll sing, too, down there by the Coosa River. We'll build a fire there by the water, because you know how dark the country can be, how dark the water is at night. And when we look back up to the dark bank, I'll tell them there's nothing to fear, even when it seems like all of Alabama is listening. You can face your fears best by acknowledging the dark, but you can always find your way back – that is, if you follow the water, or maybe even the sound of a hound baying from afar. I'll tell them that. Maybe they'll hear.

Then I'll ask them what they want to be when they grow up, and I'll say that no matter what, you have to be willing to look both ways before crossing, and that if you listen closely enough, you'll know just how far away the train is. But you just have to listen, and know your own calling. You'll hear it, even when others don't. Maybe they'll understand.

And we will taste the soil, the Coosa clay. I'll hold it up for them to see in the light, sift it through my hands to theirs. And I'll tell them the truth as I have learned it, is that we get from life more than we deserve or sometimes see, and we pass along more than we know. And because of that, there is always hope. You just have to be willing to look life squarely in its path, and not be afraid to turn away.

And maybe I'll tell some stories or just make up a few. They'll like that.

In my dream I have seen the little girl again, getting up from the piano, then standing to face me. "Do you need words? More paper?" I ask. She shakes her head and lifts up her small hand.

"No," she says, smiling for the first time. She hands me the pen, and turns away as together we close the piano case. For the first time, I know who she is and where she has been. We have journeyed together, through her journals and joys and pain. "*Fine*," she says, leaving without looking back. Perhaps she will find a cool, sweet stream where green bay leaves form a canopy overhead; or sail above the clouds to find her sister. There, they may join hands in that place called childhood, where they may play forever, undaunted.

A lake is the landscape's most beautiful and expressive feature.
It is Earth's eye, looking into which
the beholder measures the depths of his own nature.

— Henry David Thoreau

# THE END

# About the Author

Susan Shehane, a native of Millbrook, Alabama (where she was simply known as "Susie Lee"), has a masters degree in English (Secondary Education) from Auburn University Montgomery. She teaches English at Prattville Junior High School in Prattville, Alabama, and previously taught freshman composition at Auburn University Montgomery.

Twice named the recipient of the Alabama School of Fine Arts' Teacher's Award for Creative Nonfiction, she has won numerous awards for her poetry and nonfiction since 1974. As a columnist for the *Prattville Progress*, she won a national first-place award for best column in 1992, and her columns were syndicated throughout the state of Alabama in the Alabama State Employees' Newsletter. She is a former associate editor of *Bassmaster*, *Southern Outdoors*, and *Southern Saltwater* magazines. In addition, she has worked as editor of the *Montgomery Independent* as well as Auburn University Montgomery's *Filibuster*.

She is a fellow of the Sun Belt Writing Project at Auburn University, a winner of first place for graduate essay, Auburn University Montgomery, 1998, and was named to Who's Who's Among Colleges and Universities in 1996.

A lifelong resident of central Alabama, she and her husband, Dwan, moved recently to Lake Jordan. They have two adult daughters, Allison Hawkins and Stephanie Gates.

She serves as organist for the First Presbyterian Church in Wetumpka, Alabama.

Her essays have appeared in a variety of regional publications, including the former *Montgomery Magazine* and *Alabama Magazine*. This is her first published book.